FAST · AND · EASY
HOME
DECORATING

FAST · AND · EASY HOME DECORATING

An A to Z Guide to
Creating a Beautiful Home
with a Minimum of
Time and Money

ELIZABETH J. MUSHENO

ST. MARTIN'S PRESS
NEW YORK

Library of Congress Cataloging-in-Publication Data

Musheno, Elizabeth J.
Fast and easy home decorating.

1. House furnishings   2. Sewing.   3. Interior
decoration—Amateurs' manuals.   I. Title.
TX311.M86   1986   645   86–1956
ISBN 0–312–28469–1 (pbk.)

First Edition
10 9 8 7 6 5 4 3 2

Contents

A section of photographs appears following page 66.

Acknowledgments

Gratitude is due to many professional and technical people, family, and friends who gave invaluable assistance and encouragement, and lent their talents to make this book possible.

Janice Jenkins for her artistic renderings.

José Goncalves of Photo World, Denver, Colorado, who photographed my creations.

My friends and associates at the two Calico Corners decorative fabric shops in Denver and Littleton, Colorado: Ellen Jacobson, a multitalented individual who reviewed the manuscript; Bob Davis and Damia Davis-Turek, owners, who (along with their staff) shared their decorating knowledge as I conducted workshops to test the procedures.

Robin Friedman and Barbara Posner of Waverly Fabrics, Suzanne Wolf of Fabriyaz, and Bob Davis of Calico Corners.

My agent, Ray Pierre Corsini, and my editor, Barbara Anderson, for their support.

My daughter and son-in-law, Deborah and Robert Hirsch, who taught me how to use the computer and who put up with this somewhat absent-minded author as I worked on this endeavor.

FAST · AND · EASY
HOME
DECORATING

∘INTRODUCTION∘

Fast and Easy Home Decorating: An A to Z Guide to Creating a Beautiful Home with a Minimum of Time and Money, presents a new approach to decorating that will help you breeze through your next project. This alphabetized handbook offers quick ways to create new looks for every room in your home, using fabric in simplified sewn, tied-on, stapled, or glued procedures that are time-saving and economical—allowing you to assert your individual preference in interior design; eliminate the hazards of amateurish workmanship; and make decorating an enjoyable leisure-time hobby.

This book includes a commonsense approach to sewing for the home with many machine-sewn finishes that will appeal to the creative decorator who has little time for classic hand-sewn techniques. Simplified decorating is much in demand for those who want to make quick or seasonal changes. By selecting durable fabric that requires low maintenance and easy finishes that will withstand frequent cleanings, these goals may be achieved with a minimum of effort with the help of *Fast and Easy Home Decorating.*

Those who enjoy fabric crafts and who want to do their own decorating will find the step-by-step illustrated shortcuts easy to follow and foolproof. As you turn the pages of this book, you will find simple and straightforward techniques that will aid you in creating new decorative items for your home. Each technique requires a minimum amount of time and is designed to place a minimum amount of strain on your budget. With the help of this book, it will be easy to create a home with an artistic touch and pizzazz that is uniquely yours.

HOW·TO·USE·THIS ·BOOK·

Before starting any decorating project, first read the next two chapters: "Full Speed Ahead," and "You, the Decorator," and then browse through the alphabetized section to become familiar with the many procedures and terms. You will find sewing shortcuts, hints, and easy-to-make items that will help to improve your decorating skills and save you time. Use this handbook as a quick reference guide throughout each project. Study the following fabric key to understand the shading used on most of the line drawings throughout the book. Highlighted are the right side of the fabric, the wrong side of the fabric, stiffening, lining, and batting.

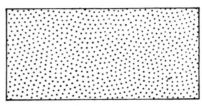

Stiffening

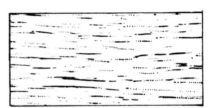

Lining

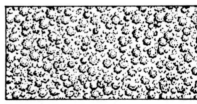

Batting

Right side of fabric

Wrong side of fabric

Speedy decorating procedures are highlighted with a hairline-rule box throughout the alphabetized section.

Pertinent suggestions appear throughout the alphabetized section to give special information. These are set off by lines and are preceded by the word "HINT."

FULL · SPEED · AHEAD

To get off to a fast start when decorating, take time to consider the following: time, money, capability, lifestyle, fabric, tools, notions, and procedures.

Be honest about your skills and the time it will take to mark, cut, and construct. If you need to work in a confined area or use "make-do" tools or work against a deadline, allow for the time needed to restore your work area to the family's needs, or for interruptions. The ideal is to have a space where your project can be left undisturbed until completed, but most people do not have that luxury. Beautiful decorating has been created in a one-room studio apartment where everything must be stored in order to open a couch for sleeping. Busy people who like to decorate always devise a way to pursue their hobby in as many steps as needed when a project cannot be completed in one day.

Step 1: Have a Plan
To move at full speed, you need a plan to save time and energy. Decorating is a very logical art form that is done with the aid of specific measurements worked out on the fabric, then cut to the requirements, without a pattern. These cut lengths of fabric are draped, shaped, and tied into beautiful masterpieces using basic tools.

Review the section on pages 9–12—a four-step evaluation list for developing a personality for your home; creating a color scheme; what to consider in each room; and how to develop a plan of action. To make an impact with your decorating skills, you will need a plan, even for the simple addition of pillows for accent or a reupholstered *chair cushion* to create a harmonious color scheme in a room that reflects your lifestyle.

Know the exact measurements of pillow forms, chair seats, windows, bed, couch, or wall—guesswork can be costly.

Careful selection of fabric, supplies, and notions will speed up construction. Having an organized work space and the appropriate tools and equipment will save time. Use the telephone Yellow Pages to locate suppliers under such listings as Draperies & Curtains (retail and custom-made), Drapery & Curtain Fixtures, Fabric Shops (retail, foam and sponge rubber), Hardware (retail), Lumber (retail), Upholsterer's Supplies, and Upholstery Fabrics (retail). Select shops in your area and plan to visit the appropriate ones personally. Phoning will not give you an overall view of the wide variety of supplies that are available for do-it-yourself decorators.

Step 2: Fast-and-Easy Fabrics

Choose an easy-to-handle fabric to speed up your decorating project. Select fabrics in solid colors, with vertical stripes, or with an all-over pattern that does not require matching. These types of fabrics will require less time during the marking, cutting, and construction steps. Prints with a predominant *pattern repeat*, plaids, checks, and horizontal stripes will require more marking and construction time. Some great designer fabrics do not require matching, and many solid-color fabrics such as gabardine, ten-ounce canvas, cobble cord or wale corduroy, petaldown, chino, denim, wool flannel, chintz, cottons or blends with all-over woven designs, and some open-weave or semisheer fabrics are easy to cut and sew. Most designer fabrics with a predominant pattern repeat and glorious English floral chintz are easy to sew after the correct lengths are cut.

Step 3: Notions

Choose notions that can save you time, speed up construction, add to the beauty of the finished project, and are serviceable.

Covered cording and piping. Available in decorator colors, these trims will save you time when you do not cut fabric strips and make your own. They can be purchased by the yard or in precut packages.

Fabric glue. Available in most shops, fabric glue is designed to work well on fabric crafts. Choose a white glue—Elmer's, Sobo, or Tacky—that dries clear. Use according to instructions on the bottle.

Fusible adhesives. The best known is Stitch Witchery. Use it instead of hand or machine stitching to bond an *appliqué, hem,* or *trim* in place. These meshlike fibers are available in 18″ widths by the yard, or in precut packages in ¾″ to 3″ widths. Fuse layers together according to product instructions.

Hammer-on snaps. Sold in packages with a tool to apply them to your fabric, hammer-on snaps may have a plain round ring or a decorative head. Use them to close the opening in a *duvet, pillow,* or any other loose opening that does not have a lot of strain exerted on it.

Iron-on mending fabric. Available in prepackaged patches or strips. Cut into the desired shape for *appliqué* or band *trim.* Adhere to foundation fabric according to package instructions.

Pleater tape with corresponding hooks. Add to unlined, lined, or sheer draperies for fast and easy *pinch pleats.* See *Draperies* procedures #1, #2, and #5.

Shirr-tape. Available by the yard in 1-cord, 2-cord, or 4-cord widths, these tapes have a heavy cord that is woven into the fabric in such a way that the cord pulls easily to form shirring or gathers. Shirr-tapes save time and eliminate the aggravation of broken threads when long edges need to be gathered to fit smaller areas. Use the 1-cord to make gathered rows to form scalloped edges on a *tablecloth* or an *Austrian shade* type of *valance.* The 2-cord type helps to make an easily gathered *dust ruffle.* The 4-cord shirr-tape is recommended for stationary draperies (see *Draperies* procedure #10) and a cloud shade (see *Roman shade* procedure #11).

Tape fasteners. These closures are jam-proof fabric strips that are stitched to each side of the opening. Nylon hook-and-loop tape fasteners, such as Velcro, are pressed together to close the opening. Snap or hook-and-eye tape fasteners are soft, flexible, and less bulky than the nylon hook-and-loop type. Tape fasteners are available by the yard or prepackaged. They may be glued or stitched in place.

Step 4: Get Organized

Organization is a key factor in speedy completion of each decorating project. Take the time to study the procedures you have selected and to collect all items needed. Decide whether you have the time to complete the project at one time, or need to plan for several segments. Either way, you will need a work space with a large flat surface for cutting; a sewing machine; iron; ironing board; measuring, marking, cutting, and sewing tools; and pressing aids.

Work space. When making bedspreads, floor-length curtains, draperies, or tablecloths, you will be using considerable yardage and may need a cutting board if you do not have the space to spread out the fabric on the floor. A ½"-thick sheet of plywood or composition board 4′ × 6′ or 4′ × 8′ on 36" to 38" high supports could serve as a cutting table. Use two ironing boards (purchased at a thrift shop), two sets of easy-to-dismantle sawhorse brackets with 2" × 4"s cut to the appropriate lengths and widths, or four chairs with backs of the same height. In some cases the cutting board must be placed over a major piece of furniture in order to have a convenient place to cut.

You may want to pad the plywood with an old blanket to prevent slippage or to protect your fabric from splinters. *Batting* and a decorative fabric could transform your cutting board into a piece of art that could be placed behind a bed or couch when not in use. Make blanket or batting 3"–4" wider and longer than the plywood and the decorative fabric 2" bigger on all edges than the padding. Staple padding to the back of the plywood along the ends and then the long side edges, leaving the corners free. Make smooth folds at the corners and cut out the excess bulk on the underside if you are covering it with fabric. Center fabric over padded plywood. On the underside, turn in the raw edges of the fabric ½" and staple in place along ends and then the long side edges. Make smooth folds at corners and staple to plywood. Think self-help and develop your own time-savers to speed up each decorating project. For example, when stitching long lengths of fabric together, support the additional weight with a card table or chair backs to eliminate extra handling and strain on the fabric that may result in crooked stitching.

Step 5: Tools and Equipment

Great decorating projects have been created with a minimum of tools and equipment, so don't purchase unnecessary gadgets. Add the required tools and equipment for each job as your skills develop. Be sure to store everything in a convenient place so you won't spend valuable time searching for misplaced items.

Measuring and marking tools. A notebook and a pen are necessary to write down all measurements that will be used to determine the amount of fabric needed.

To measure windows and large areas accurately, a 12′ retractable steel tape measure will speed up the process.

A yardstick and a 60"-long nonstretchable tape measure work best when measuring for cutting.

A carpenter's L-square will speed up marking solid-color fabrics.

A 6" metal sewing gauge is needed when measuring, marking, and pressing smaller pieces of fabric.

Masking tape is an excellent tool for making notes on fabric and for marking areas that you want to emphasize when cutting out fabric with a design motif.

Tailor's chalk or a chalk pencil may be used to draw lines and marks across the fabric. A soft lead pencil also works on the wrong side of some fabrics and will not rub off as quickly as chalk. Number off the *pattern repeats* along the selvage for accurate cut lengths.

Cutting tools. A sharp pair of bent-handled shears with 7"–8" blades will make cutting fabric easier.

Four-inch embroidery scissors or thread clips will save time when cutting threads at the sewing machine.

Sewing tools. A sewing machine in excellent condition is a necessity for many decorating projects. Thread and sewing machine needles should be selected according to the weight and type of fabric. A hinged presser foot and hinged zipper foot will expedite sewing over several layers of thick fabric. Hand-sewing needles and a thimble may be needed for some projects.

Pins come in many sizes and lengths and play an important part in decorating. Use ones that are rustproof, matching their length and thickness to the fabric. Some pins have ball points to prevent damage to delicate fabrics. Size 17 pins are about $1\frac{1}{16}''$ long and are available in fine wires for silk and delicate fabric, or in a weight called "dressmaker pins" for all-purpose use. Size 24 pins are $1\frac{1}{2}''$ long and thicker and are used for heavy fabrics such as corduroy and upholstery fabrics. Size 32 pins are about $2''$ long with plastic heads (sometimes called corsage pins) and work well when making *comforters* or when *quilting*. T-pins and pushpins are often used to hold trims or other items in place during a basting, stapling, or glueing process.

Pressing aids. Use specific pressing aids to speed up progress and obtain professional-looking results. DO NOT overpress. Use a lift-and-touch method instead of sliding the iron over the fabric. To avoid shine or ridges from the seam allowances on the right side of the fabric, do not exert pressure on the iron.

The ironing board should have a clean, smooth cover and the steam iron should be in excellent working condition.

Use a presscloth to prevent shine or iron marks on the right side of the fabric. Use a purchased presscloth or devise your own from self-fabric or muslin. If you do not have a *needleboard* for corduroy, velvet, or other napped or pile fabrics, use scraps of the self-fabric. Place the pile side of the presscloth on the right side of the fabric. Never place the iron on the right side of the pile. To press thick upholstery fabric you may need a smooth Turkish towel or washcloth for a presscloth. Be sure to test a scrap of fabric to make sure the fabric will not shrink when pressed with a dampened cloth. Press fabrics with a raised or embroidered surface over a folded Turkish towel. Place the right side down on the towel, protecting any loose threads on the wrong side with a thin presscloth.

A commercially available seam roll or wooden point presser with pounding block will help to prevent the imprint of seam allowances on the right side of the fabric. Substitute two $4''$-wide strips cut from a brown paper bag (without printing); slip strips under the seam allowances before pressing the seam open.

A tailor's ham or press mitt will help shape curves and add fullness. Substitute a tightly rolled Turkish towel to get the same results.

Spank edges into the desired shape, and pleats and gathers into soft creases or folds, with a ruler or pounding block after steaming the fabric lightly or spritzing the fabric with a spray bottle of water to avoid shine on the right side of the fabric.

Specialized tools. If you don't already have the following tools, you will need to purchase some of them for specific projects such as reupholstering chair seats or doing upholstered walls: a staple gun and staples recommended for decorating; a hot glue gun and glue sticks; pliers; narrow-nosed screwdriver; and a mat knife.

YOU, ⸰THE⸰DECORATOR

Decorating makes special demands on both time and finances, so it is important to acquaint yourself with the how-to and basic principles before plunging ahead. With an overall plan and budget in hand, and by taking time to master the required techniques, you can turn each room of your home into a pleasant, harmonious, and functional environment to complement your lifestyle.

Having worked in a large decorator fabric firm, I know firsthand some of the pitfalls that beset do-it-yourselfers. The most serious pitfall is to be a spur-of-the-moment, a no-plan, or a last-minute shopper. The spur-of-the-moment shopper first sees a fabric and then purchases it for a project without considering the rest of the room, the fabric design, color harmony, or the correct yardage. The no-plan shopper buys a sale-priced or an inexpensive fabric without considering the wear it will receive. The last-minute shopper is the person having unexpected guests who wants to spruce up the place in hours when it should take days to do the job correctly.

It's easy to make these mistakes, but it's also easy to avoid them. Before starting any home decorating project, take these four important steps and you will save yourself time, money, and heartache.

Step 1: Develop a Personality for Your Home.
To be a pleasant, functional part of your home, each room should have an element that unifies it with the rest of the house—such as harmonizing floor covering and walls. These may reflect the preference of each room's occupant.

A family room usually requires the facilities not only for relaxing but also for informal entertaining. It may have couches or futons that will accommodate overnight guests. Bedrooms, living rooms, dining rooms, and large kitchens can have quiet areas with comfortable chairs for reading, relaxing, and chatting, or they can have an area for your favorite hobby. A guest room could double (or triple) as a teenager's hideaway or as an office for the workaholic. Take time to consider your family's needs and all available options before starting a project. In every room, try to create an atmosphere that expresses your own or your family's taste. The decorator who has a home with individuality will have a feeling of satisfaction every time she enters it and her family and friends will share the enjoyment as well.

A home created for contented living requires thoughtful planning, time for shopping, and a desire to select the right item for each decorating project—at the same time staying within your budget. Many projects require only logic and limited skills while others need more research and attention to detail before starting—as well as some experience. Patience is needed when enough time has not been allowed to complete each step in decorating. If you think you can do something in five hours, you need to allow for interruptions and emergencies, so it is a good idea to double that estimate. Be realistic about your time and your skills and you will achieve the results you were aiming for.

You will achieve the best results if you do your homework and know every aspect of each room in your home, and how your latest project will visually complement the total look of your home. To develop a personality for your home, you need to establish harmonious color guidelines, working with your present furnishings.

Step 2: Create a Color Scheme.

Use an area rug, a picture, an unusual piece of furniture, wallpaper, or a length of fabric with colors that are pleasing to you to create a color scheme —and plan carefully. A good rule is to select one predominant color and then use another color or two to soften the total look. Contrasting colors should complement each other. Blends of the same color may be used for the rug, upholstery, window treatments, and walls for a monochromatic color scheme. *Accent colors* may have a more intense hue of the same color or be a sharp contrast.

Learn to analyze each color to be used, as it must contribute to a harmonious whole. Consider any new color with the color of the existing pieces— rug, draperies, bedspread, and/or upholstered furniture to make sure that the color scheme will be pleasing. For example, all hunter greens are not mixed the same way (even dye-lots vary) and some may be too yellow or too blue. Remember the *primary colors* are red, blue, and yellow, the *secondary colors* are orange, green, and purple and are made by mixing equal parts of the primary colors. The *tertiary colors* are formed by mixing equal parts of the first six colors to create six more colors. Using these twelve basic colors, each *shade, tint, value,* or *hue* is made by mixing colors and then adding the neutral-

izing colors black and gray (which appears white to the layman's eye). Colors can be made bright by retaining the original color mix, made dull by adding black, or lightened by adding gray.

Blue, green, and purple and their many shades and tints are considered *cool colors.* Red, yellow, and orange with the vast spectrum of shades are called *warm colors.*

Colors can have a physiological effect on your emotions and the way your guests feel about your home, for example:

- *Red* is stimulating and cheering and will encourage conversation and activity. It has been used in factories to increase production. Use sparingly in areas for sleeping, reading, or relaxing.
- *Blue* has an intellectual appeal and navy connotes security. It is relaxing to the nerves and has a cool, calming effect.
- *Yellow* exemplifies cheerfulness, warmth, relaxation, and has soothing qualities for the brain. Use where the room is dark.
- *Orange* can stimulate and make you feel energetic. Never use in an area where you dine— it can activate the saliva glands and cause you to overeat. Most fast-food restaurants use an abundance of orange in their color scheme.
- *Green* has a cooling effect and connotes serenity and an expression of hope.
- *Purple* has a hushing effect and is associated with valor, mystery, and passion.
- *Pinks* can have a tranquilizing effect on a hyperactive child. Painting the cell walls in bubble gum-pink paint has been used successfully in some penal institutions to help control antisocial behavior of certain inmates.
- *Blue/green* combinations can create cool, spacious surroundings that are passive.
- *Plum, mauve, orchid,* and *violet* have the same qualities as purple but in a more subdued way.
- *Brown, tan,* and *beige* may be depressing when used alone, but can exude warmth when used with other colors.
- *Black, white,* and *gray* are used to intensify other colors.

Step 3: Consider Each Room.

Put color to work in each room. After you have arrived at a color scheme, use it to bring balance to the room. Each room should be considered separately. It is not wise to start too many projects for a room—let alone a whole house—at the same time. You do need, however, some unifying aspects throughout the home: floor coverings in the form of wall-to-wall carpeting, with hard surfaces for kitchen, bathroom, and entryway in the same color may well meet this requirement. Wall colors for rooms that are open and/or connecting should be the same color, but can be of different, harmonizing shades to separate designated areas. These colors should be selected to complement you. Your favorite color is usually one that looks good on you, so it makes sense to decorate your home in your colors. *Do not* choose a color because it is trendy or because your friend used it; choose colors that reflect your preference and personality.

Determine the character and purpose of a particular room. *Quiet rooms* are needed for study, conversation, listening to music, eating, sleeping, or relaxing. *Active rooms* are for entertaining, games, or music making. *Formal rooms* are for elegant entertaining, dining, conversation, and concerts. *Casual rooms* may be all of the above and can often serve as sleeping rooms for overnight guests.

Analyze each room. Know its shape and size and the placement of windows, openings, and doors. Do the walls have structural features that may be used as a focal point, or does an area need to be camouflaged? Is there heavy traffic through the room or is it isolated? Does the room have a view to accent or does the window need to be covered? In which direction does the room face?

Examine existing furniture and the present arrangement. Does the room look balanced and pleasing to the eye? It can have a formal arrangement with the pieces being symmetrically placed or an informal look with the furniture placed asymmetrically. Formal room areas may be restful but dull if their appearance is too contrived. Don't, for example, put matching tables at either side of the bed and the same table between two matching chairs with three matching lamps. By creating a di-

version with unmatched chairs and lamps and another style table, the less formal look will carry the eyes around the entire room.

It's desirable to have small furniture for small rooms and large furniture for large rooms, but you can use colors to create an illusion if all is not in proportion. Use a slipcover with receding colors for those pieces that are too large, and use bold, bright colors to fill a sparsely furnished room.

Paint the walls the same color as the draperies to give a spacious feeling or to minimize structural flaws by using all one light, cool, or neutral color for walls and ceiling, then using bright colors on furniture to keep the eyes on the center of the room.

Each room has its own character and must have a personality that will serve the needs of its inhabitant. Color can be used to make it all work for you!

Step 4: Make a Plan of Action.

After evaluating your findings, make a permanent record that will be convenient for you to carry around when shopping for your home. Be sure to organize a space for notes on each room. Some people use a large piece of cardboard or a manila file folder for each room and carry them safely in a totebag or briefcase, others use a notebook with tabs, and some use a 3″ × 5″ index file with as many cards as needed for each room. Others carry colored photos of each wall as it is presently arranged so they know exactly what is in each room, including knickknacks. The object is to develop your own system to store paint chips, wallpaper, floor covering, and fabric swatches for each room. To be sure of the exact color, small swatches or threads of all upholstered furniture should be kept on file as well.

Measurements should be recorded for every important item. Measure height, depth, width, and length; use graph paper to make scale drawings of the following:

- Floor plans, noting every opening or alcove and exactly where it falls along each wall.
- Walls, windows, doorways, doors that swing in or out, and heating units, such as baseboards

or radiators, should be measured, as well as anything that projects into the room, such as a fireplace, or anything that is built into the wall. Make a note of the type of wall (hollow dry wall, paneling, wallpaper, etc.). Measure windows from top of window to sill, apron, and floor. Measure width and depth of indentation and width of trim.

- Ceilings that have unusual characteristics such as a beam or soffit (sometimes called a dropped ceiling) should be drawn to scale.
- Existing furniture (the area that covers the floor) should be drawn to scale, directly on your graph-paper floor plan or as separate graph-paper cutouts. Note the style and type of each piece. These will help with rearranging furniture or when you want to add something.

Next, plan a focal point that will capture the eye and invite your guests into thé room. This can be a brightly colored pillow, footstool, or painting, or an unusual statue or rug, for example.

Find out about fabric. Know how to test for durability. Ask about cleaning recommendations. Turn to *Fabric Handling* as soon as you have finished reading this section.

If at any time while compiling this file on your home you happen to get discouraged, just take a trip to some model homes or furniture stores that have complete room settings, or visit the library and browse through decorating magazines and picture books. See how carefully each detail is coordinated when executed by the professional decorator.

Now is the time to get started! Select a small project to launch yourself as a decorator. Then move on to a bigger one chosen from the ideas you'll find here. Not only will you be pleased with the outcome, but you will also receive compliments from family and friends.

WORKING ∘ PLANS ∘ FOR ∘DECORATING∘

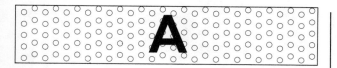

ACCENT COLOR

A single color used with a background of neutral, subdued, or pale tints to create a brilliant contrast or an intense harmonious rendering of the same background in order to amplify your color scheme.

ACCESSORIES

Decorator touches that enhance and complete the total look of a room and that should reflect your taste and personality. Use a collection of artifacts, knickknacks, books, hobby creations, a family heirloom, plants, or floral arrangement to complement or contrast with distinction. Accessories can be arranged at the whim of the decorator. Use a single object such as a curio cabinet, wall screen, musical instrument, or rug; or use a collection of objects such as a grouping of furniture, or a collection of plants. Always keep in mind a room's rhythm, balance, and harmony when using accessories.

ANCHOR

An instructional term used to remind you to hang a rod, *cornice,* etc., securely to walls or ceiling. Nails are not recommended. Use wood screws to anchor hardware to wooden trim or frame, to wall studs, ceiling joist, wood paneling, or plywood. Hollow dry walls and ceilings require special treatment.

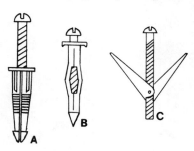

For average-weight curtains or lightweight draperies on hollow walls, use a plastic anchor (A). Make a hole with an awl, then tap the anchor in with a hammer.

For heavier draperies, cornices, valances, or shades on hollow walls, use molly bolts (B), which can be inserted with a hammer, or toggle bolts (C), which require drilled holes.

ANGLE IRON

Sometimes called a bracket or corner brace, an angle iron forms a right angle and is used to hang a *cornice, lambrequin, Roman shade,* or *valance* board. Anchor item in place as directed above.

APPLIQUÉ

A cut-out, ornamental fabric patch fastened to a larger, foundation fabric. There are several different appliqué methods, as outlined below.

1. IRON-ON MENDING PATCHES are a quick and easy method. Cut out the desired shape and *apply* to the background fabric according to package directions (A).

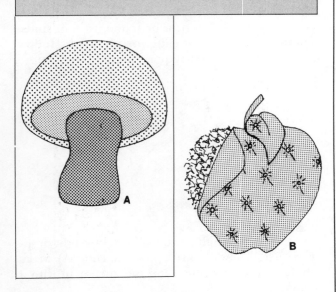

2. FUSING requires cutting out patches of fabric and the fusing agent in the same shapes. Fuse in place following manufacturer's instructions (B).

3. MACHINE APPLIQUÉ is the most durable. Cut out the desired shapes; pin or baste in place. Zigzag edges. When several layers fall in the same spot, zigzag only the top layer that shows to avoid lumps (C).

APPLY

A term used to direct you to fuse or stitch bands, ruffles, and trim at a specific time during construction.

APRON

The name given to the strip of wooden trim placed under a windowsill. Curtains and draperies are often designed to hang to the bottom edge of the apron.

AUSTRIAN SHADE

This elegant window treatment is characterized by rows of vertical shirring allowing the fabric to create soft, draping scallops. The same method is also used to make a dramatic valance. Sheer, semisheer, or lightweight fabrics that gather into soft folds work best. Add a graceful fringe and tassels or use a plain hem. Let your fabric dictate the number of scallops, the length, and the fullness as well as the hem finish.

Austrian shades may be mounted on a board or hung with a standard or continental curtain rod (See *Curtains and/or Drapery Rods*).

Austrian shades require the same consideration as Roman shades. To measure window for shade, see *Measuring Windows*. To determine yardage, see *Roman Shades*, procedure #1 for the two types of installation used; procedure #2 for the yardage work sheet with specific requirements for an Austrian shade, adding 2″ to the length measurement for a 1″ doubled hem, or ½″ for a fringe-trimmed hem (see *Casing* for requirements to hang a shade with a curtain rod, or add 3″ to mount on a board); procedure #3 for notions, lumber, and hardware, using the yardage work sheets for shade tape and cord; follow procedure #4 for mounting the finished shade.

Decide how many scallops you want for your window. When using more than one fabric width, it is important to arrange the fabric so that all seams fall under a tape; otherwise, the scallops will not hang the same.

Assemble Materials.

Fabric: Cut fabric to the predetermined width and length. Austrian shade shirr-tape: Purchase enough for each scallop, plus one extra strip. Austrian shade shirr-tape is purchased by the yard. The tape must then be cut into continuous strips, the length of the shade before shirring, and the rings must fall at the same places on each strip of tape. *Do not* purchase tape that has been seamed together, as the cords must be continuous to work. Know your cut length requirements so you can purchase individual strip yardage if necessary. Fringe: The measurement of the shade fabric width. Tassels: Same number as tape strips.

Construction.

Cut and seam fabric to desired width. Turn in side edges 1½″; press and baste. Press down top 3″ for mounting or press casing into position (A).

For a fringe hem, on right side of fabric, turn up the bottom edge ½″; press. Place top edge of fringe over raw edge, stitch both edges of fringe heading in place (B). For a plain hem, on the wrong side of fabric, turn up the bottom edge 1″; press. Turn up same amount again; stitch in place.

To attach tapes, place tapes over raw side edges 1″ from long pressed edge. Fold under bottom ends of tapes 2″; pin. Stitch securely 1½″ above the fold, continuing up one long edge of tape, being careful not to stitch over shirring cord. Stitch remaining tape edge in place (C). Stitch all tapes in place in the same manner, keeping the scallop sections evenly spaced and making sure rings are aligned horizontally across the shade.

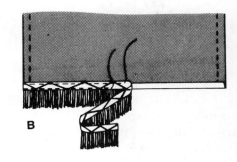

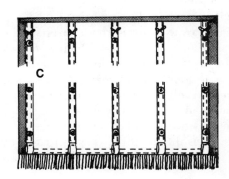

The shirr-tape has a loosely woven tube for each cord so it can be shirred easily. To have the cords free to pull after the top is completed, use a blunt-point tapestry needle to separate the loosely woven threads over the cord, then slip the needle under the cord and force out the cord end through the threads so you will be able to pull it to shirr the shade later. Pull out both cords on all tape strips at a point ½″ below where the bottom edge of the mounting board will fall, or ½″ below where the casing will be stitched.

When mounting on a board, on the right side, make a pleat at each side of all center tapes and one pleat at each side tape so shade will be the required measurement and form the scallops; pin and baste in place (D). When using a rod, stitch casing and heading in place (if being used), keeping cords free. Extra fullness should be distributed evenly along rod, between tapes, to form scallops.

To shirr the shade, pull up the two cords on each tape equally to the desired finished length, including the length of any fringe or trim. Tie cords securely at top but do not cut off. Cords may be released to clean. Distribute the shirring evenly along all the tapes, keeping the rings parallel. Sew tassels in place below each tape.

Before hanging your Austrian shade, prepare the mounting board and weight rod. Review *Roman shade* procedures #3 and #4 for directions to cover weight rod and mounting board. After weight rod has been covered, insert it through the tape loops and make all scallops evenly spaced. *Tack* each loop securely to the rod cover (E). Tie cords to tape loops, then thread cords through rings as explained in procedure #5 for the flat Roman

shade (lined), under the heading, "attach cords." Continue to follow procedure #4 to hang shade and place awning cleat to complete installation.

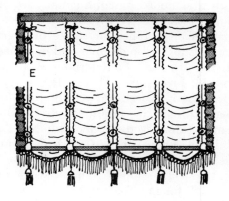

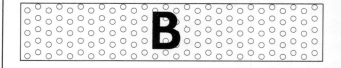

BACKING

You may have selected a light-colored fabric for a *bedspread* or *slipcover* that allows the color or design of the bed covers, or a dark upholstery print, to show through. To correct this, use an additional layer of fabric to back your decorator fabric. Backing should be a tightly woven fabric such as muslin or percale. Sheets also make good backing. Be sure the backing has the same cleaning requirements as the decorator fabric.

Cut backing to same measurement as the decorator fabric. Place wrong side of decorator fabric over the right side of backing. Machine- or pin-baste cut edges together and handle as one layer throughout construction.

BACK-STITCH

A term used for two entirely different sewing methods.

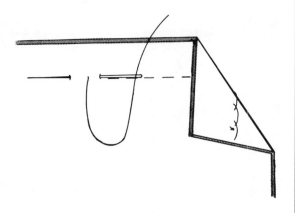

1. AS A HAND-SEWN STITCH, the back-stitch is used for repairing seams or inserting zippers. In this use, it is as strong as machine stitching. To back-stitch, knot thread, bring needle up through fabric, take a stitch about 1/16″ back, and bring needle out again 1/8″ forward. Keep taking stitches in this manner with the stitches and spaces nearly equal on the top layer and crossing over on the underside. To make the hand stitches look like machine stitches, go back into the same hole as the previous stitch.

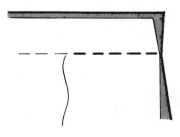

2. TO REINFORCE SEAM ENDINGS, instead of tying the thread ends, insert machine needle about ½″ from seam end. Use machine lever to stitch backward to fabric edge. Stitch forward over stitches to avoid a lump when seam is pressed open. Do the same at the opposite end of the seam.

BALLOON SHADE

See *Roman Shades,* procedure #10.

BAND TRIM

See *Trims,* procedure #1.

BASTING

A foolproof method when matching *pattern repeats* or when stitching two layers of slippery fabric. Most basting can be done by machine or with pins, but you will save time by basting by hand for certain fabrics.

1. HAND-BASTING slippery or high-pile fabrics is often the quickest way to get a smooth seam. Use a contrasting thread and long, evenly spaced stitches.

2. MACHINE-BASTING works well for holding seams and/or trim in place. Use the longest stitch length, reducing the tension if necessary for easy thread removal.

3. PIN-BASTING holds seams together or holds trim in place as you stitch. Place pins at right angle to the raw edges so you can stitch over them with a hinged presser foot. Use as many pins as needed to control the fabric or to match simple pattern repeats (A).

For seams or trims that are bulky, place pins parallel to the raw edges, with the heads facing you for easy removal (B).

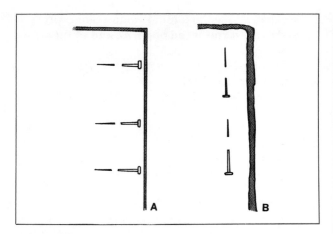

4. SLIP-BASTING is used in custom decorator workrooms to match *pattern repeats.* It is wise to trim away selvages before stitching the seam.

Working from the right side of fabric, line up the two sections along the edges to be stitched. Turn in one long edge along the line to be matched; crease and pin. Lap folded edge over the other layer, matching the pattern along lower layer; pin. Insert needle through fold on top layer, then through lower layer, keeping top layer free, making stitches on each layer about ¼ " long. On the wrong side, pull out selvage edges and stitch seam along basting.

BATHROOM

Decorating a bathroom is a challenge. Think "efficiency" as you sprinkle color and a touch of pizzazz to this utilitarian room.

1. A SHOWER CURTAIN with stationary *tie-back draperies* and a *valance* or *swag* to decorate the bathtub alcove will help to give your bathroom a classy look. (See *Draperies,* procedures #7, #8, #9, and #10.) When draping the alcove, be sure there will be enough light to see while bathing. This may seem to be an unnecessary reminder, but I've literally been in the dark because of a shower curtain and draperies.

Make your shower curtain from decorator fabric, matching the *pattern repeats,* or from a sheet. For the correct size, measure the length of the shower curtain rod and add 10″ for complete coverage and 2″ for two side hems. Then measure from the curtain hook to the point where you want the curtain to hang (usually halfway from the top of the tub to the floor) and add 6″ for top and bottom hems. Trim the plastic liner to the same dimensions, adding the 10″ for width but not allowing extra for hems. You will also need metal eyelets (grommets) and a grommet gun to insert them. You will need as many grommets as there are eyelets on your clear plastic liner. You can also make machine buttonholes instead of using grommets.

HINT: The finished decorative hem of a sheet can be used as the bottom hem. Add 3″ to finished length measurement for a top hem.

Construction.

Cut fabric to correct length and width, allowing for seams to join fabric widths and for matching pattern repeats. Stitch any seams and *clean-finish,* using procedure #4.

Turn in side edges 1″; press. Tuck in raw edges to meet fold; press and stitch in place (A). Turn up bottom edge 3″; press. Tuck in raw edge to meet fold; press. Pin and stitch bottom hem in place. Turn down top edge 3″ and complete same as bottom hem (B).

Center liner over shower curtain with upper edges even. Mark position for grommets or buttonholes through eyelets on liner. Attach grommets according to package directions or make buttonholes. Hang shower curtain on top of liner, dropping liner into tub and curtain to the outside so it will not get wet.

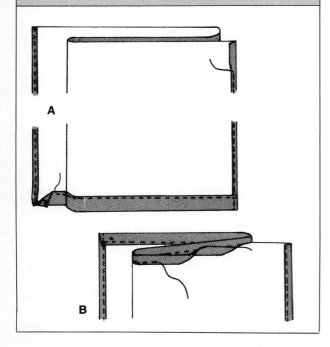

HINT: A matching or contrasting valance may be used to cover the space between the ceiling and top of shower curtain.

2 . A SINK SKIRT will give an area for storage and add a splash of color. All you need is a pair of *curtains,* with specific modifications, for the sink skirt. For a dry wall without ceramic tile, use two cup hooks and ½″-wide elastic. For ceramic walls, use a *snap tape fastener* or a *nylon tape fastener,* attached to the sink with waterproof glue, to hang the sink skirt.

For a dry wall installation, make the *casing* for the elastic with or without a heading and make the curtain as full as 1½ to 2 times the measurement from wall to wall around the sink edge and the length required. *Anchor* cup hooks to wall at each side of sink. Insert elastic into the casing with a safety pin and make it taut enough to hold the skirt in place. Stitch loops at each end of the elastic and slip over cup hooks. Presto! A super addition created with a minimum of effort.

For a ceramic wall installation, make a pair of *curtains* using a tape fastener. Make the curtain 1½ or 2 times the measurement from wall to wall around the sink, and the required length. To finish the curtain top, use the same measurements recommended for a *casing* with or without a heading. Press top of skirt down, wrong sides together, the planned amount. On the wrong side, add two rows of *gathering threads,* making the space between ¼″ narrower than the fastener strip is wide. Place the top row where the heading should start, or close to the fold. With wrong sides together, pin and gather sink skirt to fit the ball strip of the snap tape or the loop strip of the nylon tape; stitch tape to sink skirt close to both long edges of the tape. Use waterproof glue to attach the socket strip of the snap tape or the hook strip of the nylon tape fasteners at the required spot on the sink. Hang sink skirt after glue is thoroughly dry.

BATTING
A term used for fluffy sheets, made from cotton, polyester, or wool fibers, used in comforters, quilts, and cushions, or as padding for upholstered walls. In most cases bonded polyester fiberfill, high loft batting, is the best choice because of its durability. Cotton and wool batting tend to shift and need many more rows of stitches or knots to hold securely; they also do not withstand frequent cleaning.

BED LEXICON

A bed is a piece of furniture designed for sleeping, but bedrooms are rarely used just for reclining when space is at a premiun. The trick is to decorate to meet the needs of the occupant.

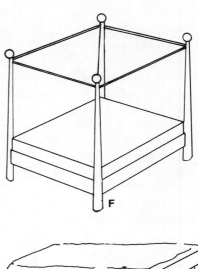

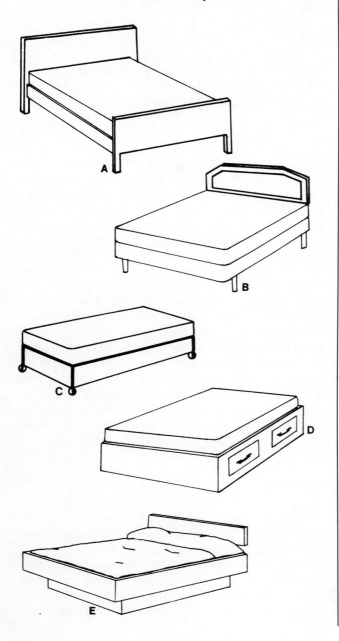

- The classic bed with a headboard and footboard is used in a traditional bedroom (A).
- The Hollywood bed with or without a headboard is more contemporary (B).
- The high-rise or twin-size Hollywood bed is most often used in a dual-purpose room, where it can serve as a couch by day and a bed at night (C).
- A captain's or platform bed often has drawers for storage and is usually equipped only with a mattress (D).
- Water beds are a blessing to the aching back and are available in both traditional and contemporary styles (E).
- The canopy bed adds old-world charm to a country, oriental, classic, or modern room (F).
- The loft bed has a place in the modern home as well as the older home with high ceilings. It is a great space saver (G).

BED LINENS

These magnificent fabric lengths of color in the form of *sheets,* pillowcases, and bedspreads are being used for all kinds of decorator touches. They may become throws for upholstered furniture, *curtains, draperies,* or *shades* and may show up in every room in the house. Be aware that sheets are not always printed on the straight grain and that it is almost impossible to match *pattern repeats.* This is an important consideration if you are planning curtains for a wide window or for several windows in the same room.

BED MEASUREMENTS

It is important to know the exact measurements for each bed. Place as many sheets and blankets on the bed as you would normally, as the bulk will affect the size of your bedspread. Use a nonstretchable tape measure and a pin, inserting the pin at the end of the tape before moving it. Bedspreads may be constructed to cover the pillows, or they may end at the headboard, using removable *pillow shams* to cover the sleeping pillows.

1. A BEDSPREAD WITH PILLOW COVERING is measured as follows: For the top length, measure from back of pillow at mattress edge, up over the pillow to the covers, tuck in 18″–24″ under pillow, and continue to mattress edge at foot of bed (A). For the top width, measure across bed from side to side. Press hand flat along side of mattress to see where the edge is with the covers in place (B). The drop length is the distance from the top edge of the bed to the floor or rug so the spread will hang free at the bottom edge (C).

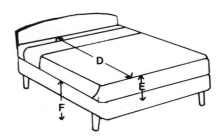

2. A BEDSPREAD WITHOUT COVERING PILLOWS is measured the same as for a bed with pillows for measurements B and C above. For the top length, measure from the head edge to the foot edge of the mattress over the covers (D).

3. FOR A COVERLET, use procedures #1 or #2 above for the top length and top width. Measure *drop* length from the top edge of the mattress to 2″–6″ below bottom of mattress (E).

4. FOR A COMFORTER OR QUILT WITHOUT PILLOW COVERING, use measurements B and D for the top width and length and measurement E for the drop length.

5. FOR A DUST RUFFLE, slide mattress away from springs. Measure from top of springs to floor or carpet to establish finished length of dust ruffle (F).

6. FOR A COUCH HIGH-RISER COVER, use procedure #2 to establish the necessary measurements.

HINT: Standard mattress sizes are listed by width × length: Twin 39″ × 75″; Double 54″ × 75″; Queen 60″ × 80″; California King 72″ × 84″, and Dual King 78″ × 84″.

The depth of the *drop* cannot be standardized as the type of frame that holds the spring and mattress

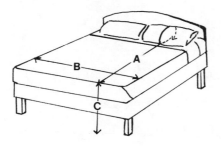

(whether it is metal or wood), the style of the bed, and the thickness of the carpet vary with each bed in each room.

BEDSPREAD FABRIC

You may select fabric that is beautiful as well as durable for a dual-purpose room or an elegant fabric that is meant to be decorative. It may be as simple or as complex as your scheme requires. Along with chintz, velvet, gingham, organdy, satin, and other classic fabrics, the fabric designers have created an unusual selection of durable printed fabrics to suit every taste. Use them plain or quilted, or use a combination of both for any room and then add matching *draperies* for a total look.

The classics such as decorator fabrics, corduroy, velveteen, fake fur, denim, and suede cloth are a good choice for heavy-duty rooms. For traditional rooms, use the elegance of a brocade, quilted satin or taffeta, dotted swiss, or any other fabric that is pretty to look at, durable, but not for lounging. Whatever the choice, be sure your bedspread will withstand the wear it will receive—your time is as valuable as the cost of the fabric. Read *Fabric Handling* before choosing fabric to aid you in making the correct purchase.

BEDSPREADS

There are two basic styles—fitted and flat—and each type has many variations and may be floor-length or a shorter version called a *coverlet* that is used with a dust ruffle. Both lengths are made the same way. Sketches show the longer length.

1. BEDSPREADS—FITTED STYLE.

This style has one common denominator with many variations. The bedspread top has a seam around the two side edges and the foot edge. It sometimes has inserted *cording* (A) or *band trim* (B), which is applied after the seam is stitched. For tops wider than your fabric, use a full width at the center with a narrower strip at each side. You may want to disguise the piecing with a gathered strip (C) or insert a contrast strip (D) to make the top section

wide enough to cover the bed. The *drop* may be floor- or coverlet-length. It may be smooth, gathered, or pleated. Smooth bands of fabric about 6″ deep may be added to the side and foot edges and then have a gathered or pleated drop for a more detailed spread.

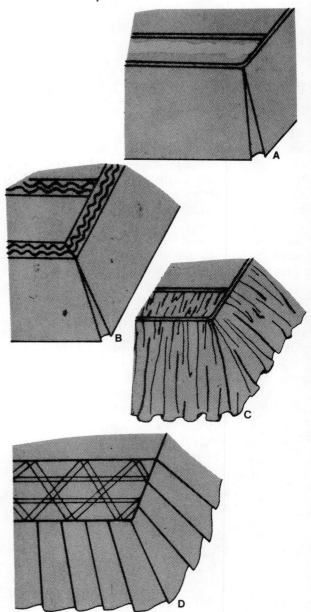

2. MAKE ROUNDED CORNERS for fitted bedspreads at the foot to prevent drooping. To make a pattern the shape of the mattress, place a heavy paper between the mattress and springs. Trace the shape, supporting the paper as you work. Cut out shape and use to shape the foot corners of the top.

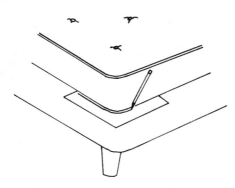

3. FITTED BOX BEDSPREAD (A). To construct, use *Bed Measurements,* procedure #4 to determine how much fabric is needed. Stitch side piecings to top if necessary.

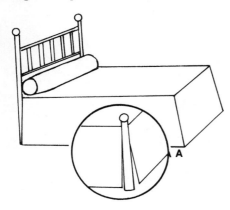

For smooth one-piece drop, stitch drop sections together. Make a 1″ finished hem, using the 1½″ hem allowance, along the bottom of the drop. Pin drop to top, allowing 2″ extra fabric along each side and 1″ extra at the foot for *ease.* Distribute ease evenly along each edge. Working from the top side, stitch

drop in place, clipping drop slightly at the corners so you can stitch more easily (B). Narrow hem head end of spread.

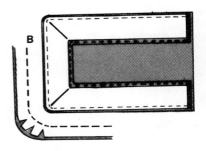

For a footboard slit, cut and seam two drop strips for the sides the length of the top plus 9½″ (2″ for ease, 7½″ for underlay). Make one strip for the length of the foot plus 4″ (1″ for ease, 3″ for two 1½″ hem allowances). Make a 1″ finished hem along the bottom and foot end of the side drop sections and a 1″ finished hem along the ends and bottom edge of the foot drop. With right sides together, pin foot drop section to the top, easing drop to fit. Pin side sections to top, lapping the finished ends 6″ over foot section, distributing ease evenly along the sides (C). Complete same as for smooth box above.

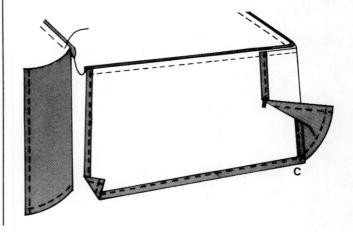

4. FITTED BEDSPREAD AND COVERLET YARDAGE WORK SHEET.

Refer to *Bed Measurements* to find the correct way to measure.

To determine number of fabric widths needed for top:

Top width (measurement B)   _____

Plus seam allowances (1¼ " total for each seam)   + _____

Equals cut bedspread width   = _____

Divided by width of fabric 36", 44", 48", 54", 60"   ÷ _____

Equals number of fabric widths   = _____

To determine cut length needed for top:

Top length (measurements A or D)   _____

Plus ⅝ " seam and 1" hem allowance   + _____

Equals top cut length   = _____

    For fabric with pattern repeat:

    Divide cut length by *pattern repeat* length   ÷ _____

    Equals number of repeats per length. If fraction remains, round up to next full number   = _____

    Multiply by length of repeat   × _____

    Equals adjusted cut length   = _____

To determine total yardage in inches for top:

Actual cut length   _____

Multiply by number of fabric widths   × _____

Equals yardage in inches for top   = _____

To determine cut length for the drop:

Drop length (measurements C or E)   _____

Plus ⅝ " seam and 1½ " hem allowance   + _____

Equals drop cut length   = _____

    For fabric with pattern repeat:

    Divide cut length by *pattern repeat* length   ÷ _____

    Equals number of repeats per length. If fraction remains, round up to next full number   = _____

    Multiply by length of repeat   × _____

    Equals adjusted cut length   = _____

To determine strip length needed for drop:

Multiply 2 times the cut length _____ × 2   = _____

Plus width of top   + _____

Equals drop perimeter   = _____

Fill in appropriate calculation for additional drop fullness for the style you are making:

For fitted box drop, add 5" for *ease,* adding another 23" for footboard slit   + · _____

For fitted box drop with corner pleats, add 29"   + _____

For a gathered drop, multiply fullness times drop perimeter: 1.5 for heavyweight, 2 times for medium weight, 2.5 for lightweight fabrics, 3 times for sheers _____ × _____, adding another 18" for footboard slits   + _____

For knife- or box-pleated drop, multiply 3 times drop circumference 3 × _____, adding another 24" for footboard slits   + _____

Note: For fewer pleats, make a pattern to determine additional fullness needed.

Drop perimeter   _____

Plus style requirements   + _____

Equals drop strip requirements in inches   = _____

Divide by fabric width   ÷ _____

Equals number of fabric widths   = _____

Actual drop cut length   _____

Times number of full fabric widths   × _____

Equals drop yardage in inches   = _____

Plus top yardage in inches   + _____

Equals total yardage in inches   = _____

Divided by 36   ÷ __36__

Equals total yardage for bedspread   = _____

Additional fabric is required for self-fabric *cording*

5. FITTED BOX BEDSPREAD WITH INVERTED CORNER PLEATS

(A). To construct, use *Bed Measurements,* procedure #2 to determine how much fabric is needed. Stitch side piecings to top if necessary.

For a one-piece drop, stitch drop sections together. Make a 1″ finished hem, using the 1½″ hem allowance along the bottom of drop. Pin drop to top, allowing 2″ extra fabric along each side, 1″ extra along the foot for *ease* and 12″ at each foot corner for pleats. Distribute ease evenly along each edge and make a 3″ inverted pleat at the corners. Pin folds in place (B). Working from the top side, stitch drop in place, clipping drop slightly at corners so you can stitch more easily. Narrow hem head end of spread. Press pleats (C).

For a footboard slit, make a mock pleat. Cut and seam two drop strips for the sides the length of the top plus 3½″ (2″ for *ease,* 1½″ for hem allowance), one strip for the foot plus 4″ (1″ for ease, 3″ for two 1½″ hem allowances), and two 9″-wide strips for pleat underlays. Make a 1″ finished hem along the bottom and foot end of the side drop sections; a 1″ finished hem along the ends and bottom of the foot drop section. Hem the side and bottom edges of the pleat underlay in the same manner. Pin drop to top with hemmed edges meeting at the foot corners; distributing ease evenly. Center pleat underlay over opening edges at foot; pin (D). Stitch drop in place and hem head end as explained above and press (E).

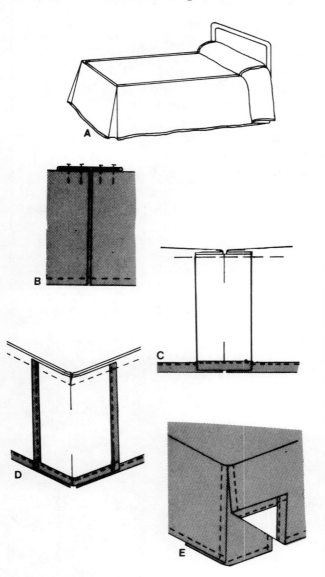

6. FITTED BEDSPREAD WITH GATHERS

(A). To construct, use *Bed Measurements,* procedure #2 to determine how much fabric is needed. Stitch side piecings to top if necessary.

For a one-piece drop, stitch drop sections together. Make a 1″ finished hem, using the 1½″ hem allowance, along the bottom of the drop. Add gathering threads at the top edge for *gathers.* Pin drop to the top along side and foot edges, distributing excess fabric evenly and allowing for extra fullness at foot corners. Adjust gathers evenly. Stitch gathered drop to top, holding top edge taut as you stitch (B). Narrow hem head end.

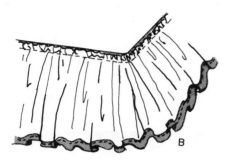

For a footboard slit, using the planned fullness, cut and seam two drop strips for the sides plus 7½″ (6″ for an underlay and a 1½″ hem allowance) and one section for the foot drop plus 3″ for the hems. Make a 1″ finished hem along the bottom and foot end of the side drop sections and a 1″ finished hem along the side and bottom edges of the foot section. Add gathering threads as above, keeping 6″ free on the side drop ends for the foot. Pin foot section to the top; distribute gathers evenly. Do the same for the sides, lapping the flat end 6″ over the gathers at the foot (C). Complete as for gathered drop above.

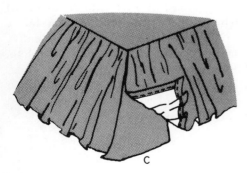

7. FITTED BEDSPREAD WITH PLEATED DROP (A). To construct, use *Bed Measurements,* procedure #2 to determine how much fabric is needed. Stitch side pieces to top if necessary.

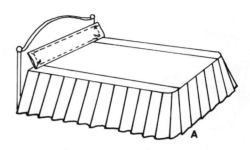

For a one-piece drop, stitch drop sections together. Make a 1″ finished hem, using the 1½″ hem allowance, along the bottom of the drop. Make *knife-edge* or *box pleats* as planned to fit the side and bottom edges; press. Pin and stitch drop to top, easing pleats to fit if necessary and keeping top fabric taut while stitching (B). Narrow hem head end.

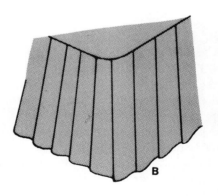

For a footboard slit, using the required amount for pleats, cut and seam two drop strips for the sides plus 7½" (6" for underlay, 1½" hem allowance), one strip for foot end plus 9" (two 3" turnbacks each with a 1½" hem allowance). Make a 1" finished hem along the bottom and foot end of the side sections and a 1" finished hem along the side and bottom edges of the foot section. Make and press pleats in side drops, keeping 6" free at the foot end and making a 3" turnback at each end of the foot drop, making sure the pleats line up at the corners. Pin foot section to top, easing pleats to fit if necessary. Do the same for the sides, lapping the underlay 6" over the folded edge of the turnback (C). Complete as for the one-piece pleated drop above.

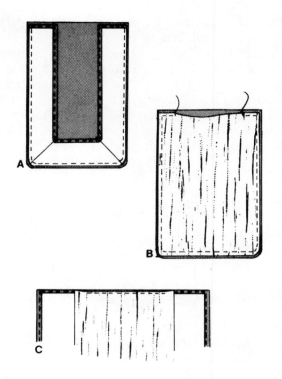

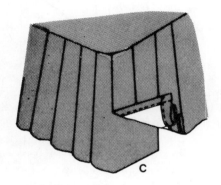

8. FITTED BEDSPREAD LINING.

To line the top, determine the yardage by using the same calculations as for the bedspread top. Piece top lining if necessary.

Before pinning drop to top, narrow hem the head ends of the drop. Pin drop in place as directed, placing ends ⅝" from head end of the top; baste (A). Pin lining over drop; stitch ends and side edges in a ⅝" seam, leaving an opening on the head end to turn bedspread right side out (B). Turn spread right side out; press. Turn in opening edges ⅝"; press. Pin folded edges together; stitch opening shut through all layers (C).

9. BEDSPREADS—FLAT STYLE.

These easy-to-make bed toppers are called by many names. Designed to be used on a bed without a footboard, the flat floor-length is called a *throw* and the shorter style used with a dust ruffle is called a *coverlet. Comforters* are used as coverlets, while quilts may be either floor or coverlet length. These simple bedspreads can be as plain or as fancy as your heart desires. Make your own design by decorating the edges with *cording, ruffles,* or *trims.* Add the luxury of quilting, patchwork, or appliqué, or let the fabric tell the decorating story. Whatever your creative instincts, a flat bedspread will be easy to complete. Stitch the hem in place by machine, or use a lining. Remember, when piecing, use a full fabric width at the center of the spread with a narrower strip at each side to accommodate the width required.

10. FLAT FLOOR-LENGTH THROW AND COVERLET YARDAGE

WORK SHEET: Refer to *Bed Measurements* to find the correct way to measure.

To determine number of fabric widths needed:

Top width (measurement B)		_____
Plus drop lengths (measurements C or E) _____ $\times$ 2	+	_____
Plus four ⅝″ seam allowances	+	2½″
Plus 3″ for two 1½″ hem allowances for unlined—or—1¼″ for lined	+	_____
Equals total cut bedspread width	=	_____
Divided by width of fabric 36″, 44″, 48″, 54″, 60″	÷	_____
Equals number of fabric widths needed	=	_____

To determine cut length for each width:

Top length (measurement A or D)		_____
Plus drop length	+	_____
Plus 2½″ hem allowances (1″ for head, 1½″ for foot) for unlined—or—1¼″ for two ⅝″ seam allowances	+	_____
Equals cut length	=	_____

For fabric with pattern repeat:

Divide cut length by *pattern repeat* length	÷	_____
Equals number of repeats per length. If fraction remains, round up to next full number	=	_____
Multiply by length of repeat	$\times$	_____
Equals adjusted cut length	=	_____

Your actual cut length measurement		_____
Times number of fabric widths	$\times$	_____
Equals yardage in inches	=	_____
Divided by 36	÷	36
Equals total yards required	=	_____

11. FLAT THROW OR COVERLET—UNLINED.

A throw and a coverlet are made the same way. The throw is the longer length (A). To make a dust ruffle for your coverlet (B), see *Dust Ruffle.*

Stitch the two narrower sections to the full fabric width center. *Clean-finish* seam allowances if necessary.

To round corners for the foot end, use the measurement of the drop plus the hem allowance. Where the side and foot measurements intersect, mark the corner point with a pin or make a dot with chalk or a soft lead pencil. Use a yardstick and pivot it at the intersecting mark; move it about an inch at a time along the corner edges to be rounded and draw a short line at the end of the yardstick as it is moved. Shape the marks into a smooth rounded line and cut off excess fabric (C). Make a 1″ finished hem on the side and foot edges, using a 1½″ hem allowance. (For help with the rounded corner, see *Hems,* procedure #1.) Narrow hem head end of spread.

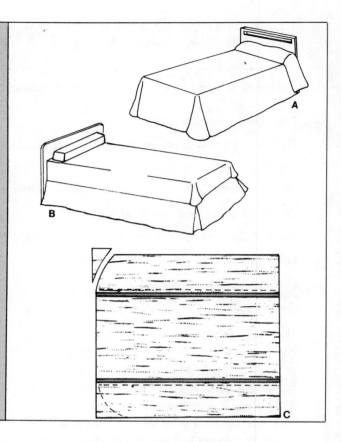

12. FLAT THROW OR COVERLET—LINED:

Stitch bedspread sections together and round corners as for unlined style above. Cut and stitch lining seams as for bedspread. Press all seams open; do not *clean-finish.*

With right sides together, stitch lining to spread in a ⅝″ seam, leaving an opening at the head end to turn right side out (A). *Trim* corners and curves to eliminate bulk. Turn right side out; press, turning in opening edges ⅝″. Pin folded edges together and stitch through all thicknesses (B).

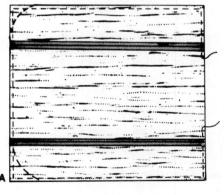

BIAS

A diagonal line across the lengthwise and crosswise grain of fabric is called bias grain. Since many of today's manufacturing techniques distort the fabric grain during the finishing process, you may not be able to achieve a true bias. Soil release, permanent press, and polished cottons must be used "as is." Do not be concerned as the bias strips cut from these fabrics will work up beautifully. When making self-fabric or contrasting *cording ruffles,* or band *trims,* many decorators let the fabric's design dictate whether *straight grain strips* (lengthwise or crosswise) or bias strips will be used. When making *bias binding,* the fabric must always be cut on the bias as directed in procedures #1 or #2 below.

To cut bias strips, start by straightening one corner or both edges across the fabric, making it at right angle (perpendicular) to the selvage. Fold corner diagonally; crease. Mark crease line with ruler and a soft lead pencil on the wrong side of the fabric. Use leftover fabric for small projects. For larger quantities such as a corded bedspread hem, it is easier and quicker to purchase additional fabric to make continuous strips.

1. TO USE LEFTOVER FABRIC,

straighten one corner and mark as directed above. Draw as many strips of the desired width as needed, allowing ¼″ at each end for piecing. Draw all ends along the straight grain. Cut along markings (A).

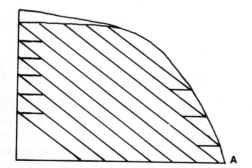

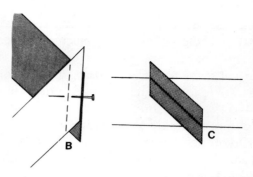

Join strips together at the short ends by placing right sides together with cut edges even. Pin and stitch where strips intersect, usually ¼″ from ends as shown (B). Make strips as long as needed; press seams open (C).

2. FOR CONTINUOUS STRIPS,

straighten both edges between the selvages and mark corner as directed above. Draw strips of the desired width, ending at the opposite corner. Cut away corners along first and last strip line (A).

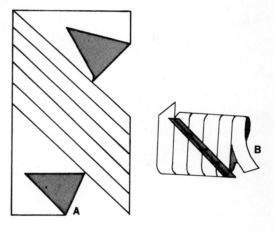

With right sides together, pin strip ends together, matching lines and with one strip extending beyond the ends at each side. Stitch in a ¼″ seam; press seam open. Start cutting along marking at one end (B). When cutting is completed you will have one continuous strip.

HINT: To help estimate how much extra yardage will be needed for self- or contrasting fabric bias cut strips to make *cording, binding,* or *trim,* use the following guide: A ½ yard length of 48"–54" wide fabric will yield a 2" wide bias strip approximately 5 yards long; a 1 yard length, a 10 yard long bias strip; a 1½ yard length, an 18 yard long bias strip, a 2 yard length, a 26 yard long bias strip.

BIAS BINDING

This handsome finish is a way to eliminate a facing or hem. Use purchased double-fold bias tape or make your own. Bias binding may be as narrow as ¼" or as wide as 2". To make your own, use *bias* procedures #1 or #2 as directed above.

Make strips four times the desired width, plus ⅛"–¼" for shaping (thicker fabric will need the most). Cut enough strips to cover the edge(s) to be bound, piecing as needed. Allow 2" to finish the ends. Example: For a ¼"-wide binding you need strips 1" wide plus ⅛"–¼" for shaping. For a 2"-wide binding you need 8"-wide strips plus ⅛"–¼" for shaping.

1. TO FORM BINDING, fold strip in half, wrong sides together; press, stretching gently to remove *slack.* (A). Open strip and turn in cut edges toward the crease, making the bottom layer a scant ⅛" wider than the top layer; press lightly (B).

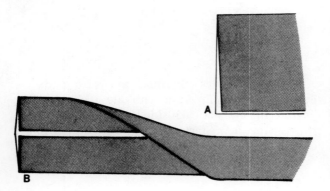

2. TO STITCH BINDING TO AN EDGE, open binding and pin narrowest edge to the right side of the edge to be bound, making the raw edges even. Stitch binding in place along crease (A). Turn binding to the wrong side along the stitching, encasing the raw edges. Make sure the remaining folded edge covers the seam stitching a scant ⅛"; pin. On the right side, stitch in the groove where the binding joins the fabric, catching in the bottom free edge in the stitching (B).

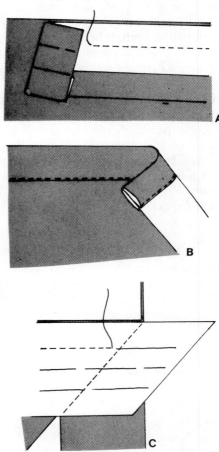

To make strips continuous, stitch ends in a seam or lap them. For a seam, keep 1" of the strip free at the beginning of the stitching (see step A above). When you have stitched to within 1" of the beginning, stop and break the threads. Fold edge so the binding ends are at right angles. Stitch along the straight grain where they meet, keeping the edge being bound free. Trim seam allowances to ¼″ (C). Press seam open and complete stitching (D). Finish binding as in step B above.

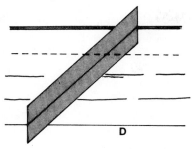

For lapped ends, turn in the beginning end ½″ and stitch binding in place as for step A above. When you come to the turned-in end, allow ¾″ to lap over it and complete the stitching (E). Finish binding as in step B above.

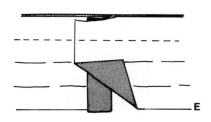

3. TO BIND A CURVED EDGE, the binding (both purchased and self-made) must be shaped to match the curve on a circular tablecloth, scalloped trim, etc. Use a steam iron and press lightly.

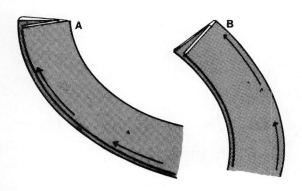

For an inward curve, stretch the two folded edges while easing the single folded edge (A).

For an outward curve, stretch the single folded edge while easing the two folded edges (B).

4. TO BIND OUTWARD CORNERS, end stitching the same distance from the opposite edge as the binding is wide (A). Fold binding diagonally and extend the strip upward. Make another fold so the strip is even with the opposite side of the corner; stitch folds and binding strip in place following the crease (B). Turn binding to inside forming a smooth *miter* on the front (C). On the wrong side, form another miter, placing the fold in the opposite direction from those on the right side so you won't have a lumpy corner. Pin and stitch free edge in place following procedure #2 above (D).

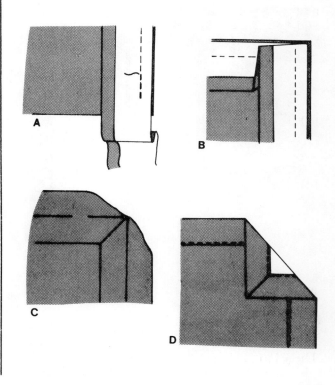

5. TO BIND INWARD CORNERS,
make a row of reinforcement stitches the same distance as the finished binding width about 1″ on each side of the corner. Clip to stitching at corner (A). When stitching the binding in place, open the corner so the reinforcement stitches are in a straight line. Stitch along the outside of the stitches so they won't show when the binding is completed (B). On the wrong side, pull *miter* through clip (C). Make another miter placing the folds in the opposite direction on the remaining edge. Pin and stitch entire free edge in place following procedure #2 above (D).

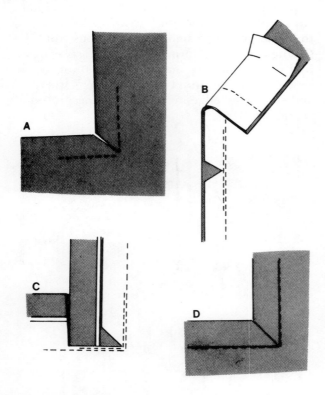

BLIND-STITCH
See *Hemming Stitches*

BOLSTERS
These long thin cylindrical-, box-, or wedge-shaped cushions are used for back support on couches. Today bolsters are also used on beds or in a softer form as pillows for *accent color.* Support cushions are firm and the forms are made of foamlike shapes or a combination of foam and batting for a softer look. Decorative pillows are softer and can take the shape of a long pillow for your bed, instead of the traditional two-pillow topping. Soft, short, round bolster pillows make excellent neck rolls.

BOLSTER COVERS
Use bolsters to transform a high-rise, Hollywood-style twin-size bed, or a daybed into a comfortable couch. Only the shape makes the bolster different from the classic *box-edge cushion* found on a regular couch or chair. Make bolster covers to match or contrast with your *bedspread* or *couch cover.*

Purchase bolster forms or make your own from an old white sheet or muslin stuffed with foam chips, polyester fiberfill, or a combination of foam with *batting* wrapped around it.

HINT: When making a pair of covers, do the same step for each as you work.

---

1. A ROUND BOLSTER COVER may have a plain seam at the ends or it may be ruffled, fringed, corded, or have decorative trim. Ends may be gathered with a button or tassel at the center or tied.

Measure the length and circumference of the form. Measure diameter of ends (A). Add 1¼″ to all measurements for two ⅝″ seam allowances.

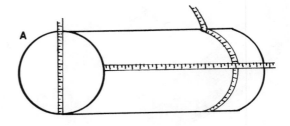

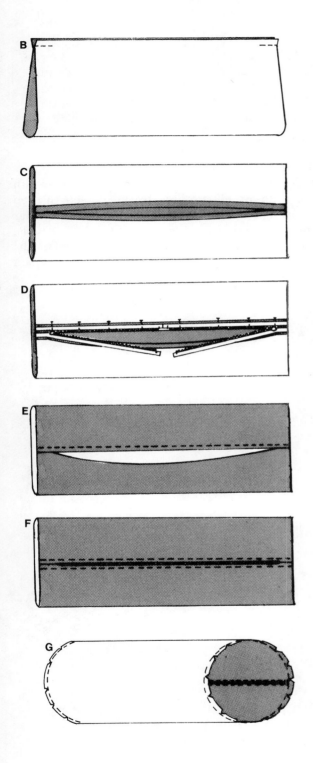

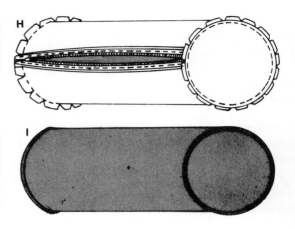

Cut out long cover and both end pieces. (Cut *bias* or *straight-grain strips* for self-cording if desired). The *slip-stitch* closure is the least expensive, but I prefer to use a zipper closure for the large backrest type of bolster as it is faster and less aggravating. If you can't find a zipper long enough (usually 36″), use two 18″-zippers.

To insert zipper, fold long cover piece with right sides together and stitch longest edges together at each end for 1″ in a ⅝″ seam (B). Press seams open, continuing across opening and being careful not to stretch the fabric (C). Open zipper(s). Center face down over one opening edge, with stop(s) ¾″ from end(s). (Pull tabs should meet at center of opening when using two zippers.) Pin one tape in place with teeth along opening edge; overlap tape ends where they meet at the center when using two (D). Using a zipper foot, work through opening; stitch along center of tape about ¼″ from pressed opening edge (E). Close zipper(s). Pin remaining opening edge to zipper tape with pressed edges meeting. Open zipper(s) and stitch pinned tape in place (F).

Note: Due to the confined area of this long narrow tube of fabric, the above method of zipper application was selected as the easiest for all fabrics. If you wish to baste the opening shut, press the seam open, and stitch the zipper(s) in place over the basted opening. Center zipper(s) face down over the basted seam; pin. Using the zipper foot, stitch zipper(s) in place along the center of each tape and across the ends. Remove basting.

Add *reinforcement stitches* ½″ from both ends of tube. Clip at even intervals to stitching (G). Baste trim, if being used, to circles at this time. Follow *cording*, procedure #3, clipping the cording seam allowances only enough so they will lie flat and make the cording continuous.

   Open zipper(s). With right sides together, pin ends to tube, spreading clipped seam allowance as you pin, keeping raw edges even. Stitch from the tube side, inside the reinforcement stitches (H). Turn right side out through zipper opening. Shape ends smoothly and insert forms (I).

2. BONBON BOLSTER COVER: this may be soft or firm and with or without a zipper. Measure form as for procedure #1, step A above. Make fabric about 20″ longer than form and cut two strips 2″ wide and 8″ long if you want self-fabric bands.

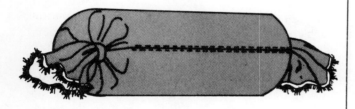

For the classic zippered cover, insert zipper as for procedure #1, steps B through F above, stitching the ends for about 8″. Finish ends with a decorative hem as explained in *Trims*. With a sturdy thread, add two rows (1″ apart) of gathering threads where the fabric should gather to form the ends (see *Gathers*). Pull up gathering threads as tight as possible; fasten securely. Turn in long edges of strips to meet; press. *Slip-stitch* strip over gathers at each end, turning in raw ends where they meet. Slip-stitch ends together.

For a quick and easy cover, cut as directed above. Stitch seam to form tube. Finish ends with a decorative hem as explained in *Trims* or make *fringe*. Insert form and gather ends together with ribbon or cord.

3. WEDGE-SHAPED BOLSTER COVERS: these are most often decorated with plain ends or self-cording. Measure the length; then measure up one side, across top, down the other side, and across the bottom for width. For ends, measure height and both top and bottom widths (A). Add 1¼″ to all measurements for two ⅝″ seam allowances.

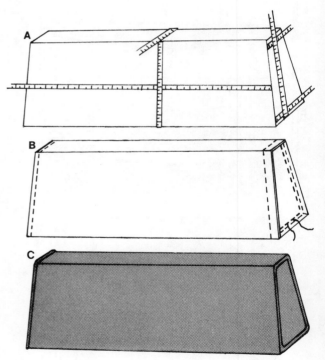

Cut out long cover section and both end pieces. Make *cording* first, if being used, and baste to ends. Insert zipper in long cover section following procedure #1, steps B through F above.

Add *reinforcement stitches* ½" from both ends. Open zipper(s). With right sides together, pin ends to tube, placing zipper closure on the back bottom edge; clip tube at corners as you pin, keeping raw edges even. Stitch from the tube side, just inside the reinforcement stitches (B). Turn right side out through zipper opening. Shape ends and insert form (C).

BOLTS

The most common bolts a home decorator will encounter are *anchor* devices called molly bolts and toggle bolts. They are used to hang *drapery rods, cornices,* etc.

BOX-EDGE CUSHION

This cushion is most often seen on upholstered or wicker furniture, outdoor furniture, and all kinds of benches and window seats. They are usually square or rectangular, but some are round and others are shaped to fit the contours of the seat. The classic style has *cording* on both edges of the box. Two newcomers to the decorator scene are the smooth box and the Turkish-corner box, which are made from two flat fabric pieces.

Use a purchased form or make your own out of an old white sheet or muslin with foam chips, polyester fiberfill stuffing, or a combination of foam with *batting* wrapped around it.

1. CLASSIC BOX-EDGE CUSHION COVER
For square and rectangular forms, measure length, width, height, and then around the form for boxing strip length (A). For round forms, measure diameter, height, and then around the form for boxing strip length (B). Add 1¼" to all measurements for two ⅝" seam allowances.

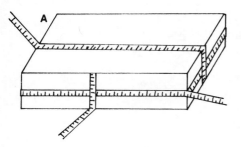

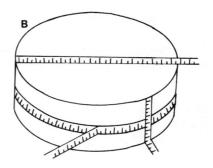

You can make a pattern for the top and bottom by tracing along the edge of the form and then adding a ⅝" seam allowance on all edges. Do the same for the boxing strip. Using pattern, cut out two fabric pieces and the boxing strip less the zipper length. Cut out the remainder of the boxing strip as explained in step C below. Make *cording* (if being used) twice as long as the boxing strip measurement and baste to top and bottom sections.

The zipper closure is nearly invisible. For squares or rectangles, use a zipper 2"–4" longer than one edge. For a round form, use a zipper at least ⅓ the length of the boxing strip. Cut a strip as long as the zipper tapes and 1½" wider than the boxing strip (including the seam allowances). Cut strip in half lengthwise, *machine-baste* strips together in a ¾" seam, and press open. Center zipper face down over basted seam. Using zipper foot, stitch along center of each zipper tape. Remove basting (C). Stitch zipper strip to boxing strip; press seam away from zipper.

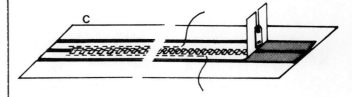

For a cushion with corners, center zipper over one edge, leaving 2" free. Stitch top to strip, keeping edges even and stitching ⅝" from edge. At each corner, stitch to within ⅝" of next side; with needle in fabric, raise presser foot and clip strip to needle.

Pivot fabric on needle until next side is lined up. Make sure strip and top are flat so fabric won't pucker. Stitch remainder of strip in place in this manner, stopping about 2″ from other end (D).

For a round cushion, make reinforcement stitches ½″ from each long edge of strip. Clip to stitching at even intervals. Starting with the zipper section, stitch top to strip, keeping 2″ free and spreading clips so the raw edges are even. Use a ⅝″ seam so stitching is inside the reinforcement stitches, stopping 2″ from other end (E).

For either style, join strip ends in a seam ⅝″ from zipper section, allowing enough strip fabric to complete boxing (F). Turn seam away from zipper and complete stitching. Open zipper and stitch bottom to boxing strip in same manner, lining up edges with top (G). Turn right side out and shape cover. Insert form (H).

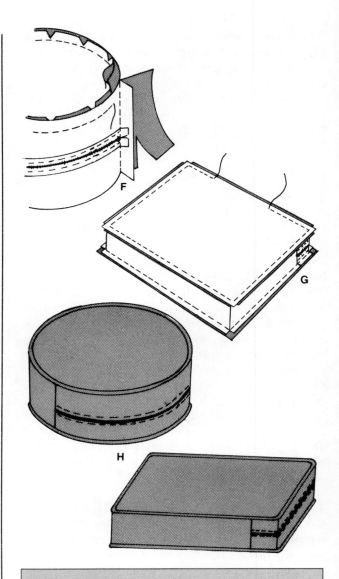

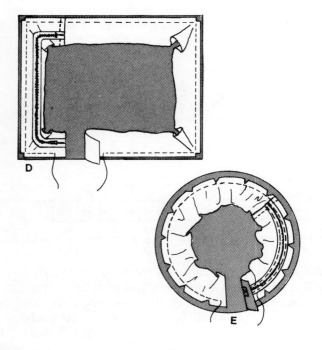

2. **QUICK BOX-EDGE CUSHION COVER.** This method can be used only for square or rectangular cushion forms. Measure form as explained in procedure #1, step A above. To both the length and width measurements add the height of the box plus 1¼″ for two ⅝″ seam allowances. Example: For a 14″ × 3″ rectangular cushion form, add 4¼″ to each measurement. Cut out two fabric sections 18¼″ square.

Openings may be *slip-stitched* or zippered shut. The zipper should be the same measurement as the cushion. To insert a zipper, join the two fabric sections together at each end of the closure seam, one-half the measurement of the box, in a ⅝" seam. *Machine-baste* opening shut; press open (A). Center zipper, face down, over basted seam; with zipper stop at end of one seam; pin. (Excess zipper tapes can be trimmed off after cushion ends have been stitched.) Stitch in place through the center of the zipper tape and across both ends (B). Remove basting. Open zipper. Stitch sides and remaining end in a ⅝" seam, beginning and ending 1" from edges. Press seams open (C).

To make each corner, bring seams together, forming a point, and match seam lines. Mark a seam where base of triangle is the same measurement as the cushion height. Stitch between folds to form corner; trim to ⅝" (D). Turn right side out and shape corners; insert form (E).

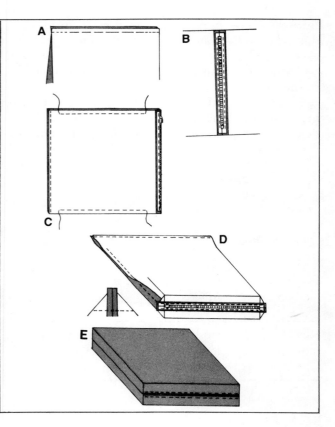

3. TURKISH-CORNER BOX-EDGE CUSHION COVER.

Sometimes called butterfly corners, this style can be used only for square or rectangular box-shaped cushion forms. You may want to soften a foam form with a wrapping of *batting.*

Measure and cut top and bottom sections as explained for procedure #2 above.

Mark both sections at each corner with *tailor's chalk,* forming squares with chalk as shown. Example: For a 3"-deep box, make a 2⅛" square (1½" for one-half the box depth, ⅝" for seam allowance). Now draw a line through the apex of the square (A).

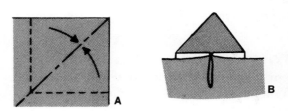

To shape, crease along the outer lines as shown; bring together over center line, forming pleats. Stitch pleats in place ½" from raw edges (B). Trim away extending fabric. Prepare pleats and stitch remaining corners on both sections.

Insert zipper in one seam as directed in procedure #2, steps A and B above, matching pleats at corners, using a zipper the length of the form. Or *slip-stitch* the opening shut after the top is stitched to the bottom.

Stitch top to bottom, leaving an opening for turning and matching all corner pleats, using the desired closure. Turn cover right side out, shaping corners. Insert form (C). Secure closure.

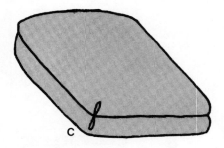

HINT: *Cording* may be inserted in the seam for a more tailored look. I use a slip-stitched closure with cording to avoid hassling with a zipper.

BOX PLEAT

A double pleat that has wide folds on top and narrower folds underneath. Box pleats are used in *draperies, bedspreads, couch covers, dust ruffles,* and skirts on upholstered chairs and couches. To use box pleats, see *Draperies,* procedure #4 for self-pleated headings, and procedure #9 for tab hanger stationary draperies.

BOXING STRIP

A long narrow fabric strip used on *box-edge cushions* to form the depth to accommodate a boxlike form.

BRAID

A flat, narrow band of trimming that is braided or woven. This is a favorite decorator touch that can be sewn or glued in place or used for *tiebacks,* to hold cascades, etc.

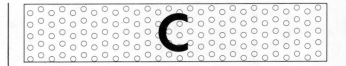

CANOPY

At one time, a canopy was considered utilitarian. In cold weather it framed an entire bed to help prevent body heat from escaping; in hot weather thin netting was used to keep the insects out and allow the air to flow through. Today's canopies are used to decorate a sitting or sleeping area. They can be suspended from supports projecting from the wall or they can be attached to the ceiling. Canopies can frame just the head or the entire length of a bed or couch. For a modern approach, they can be formed by draping luxurious lengths of fabric through rings hung from the ceiling.

Throughout this book you will find many types of *curtains, draperies, cornices, swags,* and *valances* that can start you on an adventure to make a one-of-a-kind canopy.

CARTRIDGE PLEAT

This pleat gets its name from the cartridge belt that soldiers use to hold extra ammunition. To make cartridge pleats see *Draperies,* procedure #4 for self-pleated headings.

CASING

A layer of fabric turned to the underside of a curtain, then stitched in place allowing for a rod to be inserted to hang a curtain. Sometimes called a tunnel or a rod pocket, a casing can also be used to accommodate elastic or drawstring that will gather fabric to fit a smaller area. A plain casing (procedure #1 below) is most often used on curtains when their tops are to be covered with *draperies, cornices,* etc. A casing with a heading (procedure #2 below) will form a decorative edge above the top of the rod and is often a design feature for special window treatments. Use either style casing for stationary *draperies* to hang them with regular or decorative rods. Make a casing the same way you would a hem—after the sides of each panel are hemmed.

A casing with a heading will form a ruffle above the curtain rod. For sheers, use a ½″–1″-deep heading. The rule of thumb for decorator fabric is: the longer the draperies, the deeper the heading may be. Example: When using a 4″ PVC pipe or a continental rod to hang floor-length stationary *draperies,* you could use up to a 4″ heading successfully.

1 . C A S I N G . Adjust the width of the casing to accommodate the rod where necessary, adding the casing requirements to the finished length desired. For a standard curtain rod, use 2″. Turn down the top edge 2″ (after the side hems have been made); press. Turn in the raw edge ½″; press and pin, making sure the ends do not show on the right side of the curtain. Stitch inner edge in place (A). Insert rod through casing, forming gathers. Hang; distribute fullness evenly along the rod.

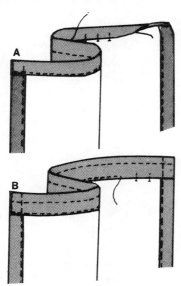

2 . C A S I N G   W I T H   H E A D I N G . Determine how deep to make the heading and adjust the casing width to accommodate the rod. Example: For a standard curtain rod use at least a

1″ heading and 2″ for the casing. To the finished length requirement, add 4″ (2″ for the 1″ heading that is doubled above the rod, 2″ for casing).

To make the casing with a heading, turn down the top edge one-half the predetermined heading width plus the casing width or 3″ (1″ for the heading is added to the finished length on the right side of the curtain that will extend above the rod, plus 2″ for the casing); pin and press. Stitch 1″ from fold to form heading. Turn in raw edge ½″; press and pin, making sure the ends do not show on the right side of the curtain. Stitch inner edge in place (B). Insert rod through casing, forming gathers along the rod and a heading (ruffle) above the rod. Distribute gathers evenly after the curtain is hung.

CHAIR CUSHIONS
There are several ways to change the look of your chair seats: make loose cushions that tie on using the *box-edge cushion* or the *knife-edge pillow* style; reupholster the seat; make a slipcover.

1 . L O O S E   T I E - O N   C U S H I O N S . Make a pattern by taping an opened paper bag in place over the seat. Carefully make a "rubbing" around the seat edge by using the side edge of a soft lead pencil. Mark position of back and arm supports where the cushion will be tied on. Use pattern to make a form the same size as the seat out of ½″–1″-thick foam. It may be made softer with a wrapping of *batting.* Add ¾″ to all edges for a ⅝″ seam and ⅛″ take-up allowance for the form.

Cut out top and bottom, using *cording, ruffles,* or *trim* basted to one section before adding ties. For a large bowtie, use a strip 5″ wide and about 54″ long. Stitch ends together; then narrow hem the long edges in one continuous operation. For narrow ties, use a strip 2½″ wide and about 48″ long. Fold in half lengthwise; stitch ends and long edge in a ¼″ seam, leaving an opening to turn. Turn right side out; press. Stitch opening shut.

For either style tie, baste ties at marks, pleating in width as necessary (A). Complete cushion following directions for a *box-edge cushion* or a *knife-edge pillow cover.* Tie cushion in place (B).

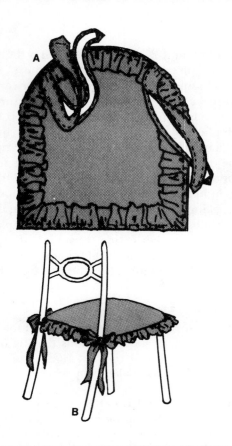

HINT: Use cords with tassels or ribbon for quick ties.

2. REUPHOLSTER CHAIR SEATS.

Measure each chair separately even though they all appear to be identical. Remove seat and examine how it is covered. A new layer of *batting* or thin foam will add to the overall beauty of the newly covered seats.

For a plain, smooth cover, measure at the deepest point from the front edge to the back of the seat, including the wrap and the extension of the cover that is stapled in place. Do the same at the widest part of the seat.

For a box-edged cover, measure from the front seam edge to the seam at the back and across the widest part of the seat. Measure the depth and length of the boxing strip, including the amount pulled to the underside.

For both types, use the old cover as a pattern, allowing a little extra around all edges as the fabric may have shrunk over years of use. Make a tentative layout, drawing in the amount of seat and boxing sections you need. See *Bias,* procedure #2 to estimate yardage needed for cording.

To upholster seat, remove seat from chair and tape screws securely to each chair (A). Remove old covering with chisel or screwdriver, being careful not to tear fabric (B). Cut out new fabric, using old cover, centering a design motif for each seat as dictated by your fabric.

Center seat over wrong side of the new upholstery fabric with the padded side down. Starting with the front edge, pull fabric up over the padding to the wooden base and staple at the center about ½" from the fabric edge. Next, gently pull the fabric taut at the back edge; staple. Now secure the center of each side in the same manner (C).

Check right side of the seat to make sure any design is centered. Staple the front edge to within 1"–2" of each corner, keeping fabric smooth and staples close together. Then staple the back in the same manner, keeping fabric taut. Make tiny pleats along a curved edge and staple so the folds are flat. Do the sides in the same manner. At the corners, pull fabric taut at the longest edge; staple. Make as many pleated folds as necessary at each corner so the fabric is flat on the underside without making puckers or dimples on the upholstered side (D).

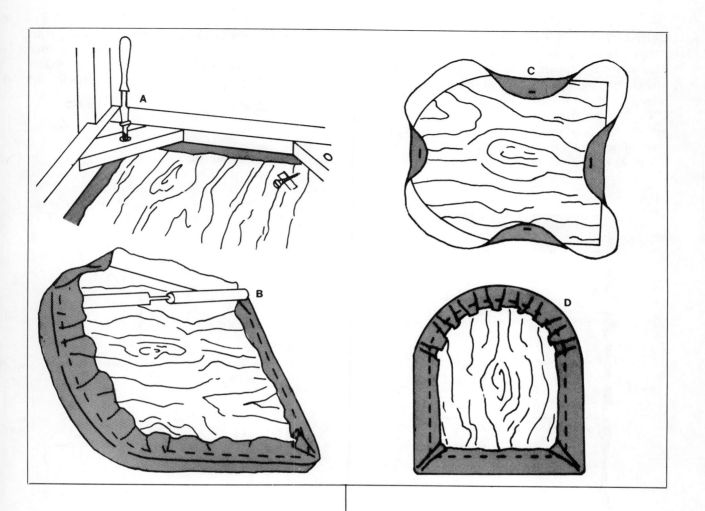

3 . S L I P C O V E R . Make simple one-piece covers that are tied on to change color or add pizzazz. Use one layer of fabric; shape to fit the contours of the seat, allowing 1″ extra around the bottom for a hem, marking position of back, arms, and legs so the slipcover can be tied in place at the back and front of the seat. For chairs with box-edge cushions, you may want to make square corners as shown for *Box-edge Cushions*, procedure #2 or #3. Narrow hem the edges, finish with *cording* or a *ruffle* (gathered or pleated). Make ties as suggested above or make short *tabs* with a snap or button for easy removal that will hold the slipcover in place.

CHALK
There is a chalk called tailor's chalk made specifically for use on fabric. Use it to make lines or marks on either the right or wrong side of the fabric.

CLEAN-FINISH

A term directing you to finish the free edges of a hem or seam allowance that may ravel, fray, or be unsightly. The following clean-finish methods are recommended for decorating:

To clean-finish the raw edges of a seam allowance or the edge of a hem before it is stitched in place, turn under the raw edge ¼"; stitch (A). Stitch ¼" from the raw edge (B), or zigzag it (C).

To clean-finish seam allowances together, trim seam allowances to ¼"; zigzag cut edges together (D). Or make a mock French seam by tucking in the raw edges to meet the seam and stitch the folded edges together (E).

CLIP

Short snips made in the seam allowance after the seam has been stitched or when a curve or corner is reinforced. Clip just to the line of stitching, but not through the stitching, so the seam allowances will lie flat, or to allow for special handling.

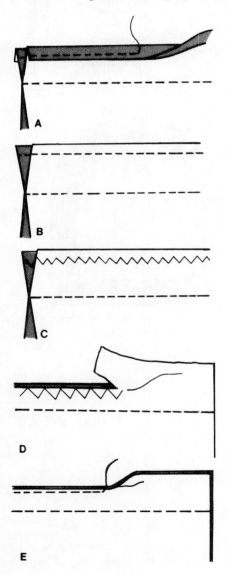

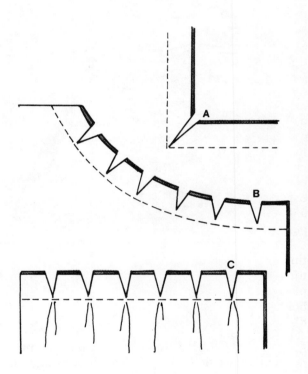

Clip to line of stitching at corners (A). Clip inward curves at even intervals (B). To see if you have clipped enough, hold fabric at each end of the seam; it should stretch out in a straight line (C). If the seam allowance curls, more clips are needed.

CLOSURE

Any method that is used to close an opening required to turn an item right side out or for an item to be opened to slip on easily and then closed after it is in place. See *Slip-stitch* for a hand-sewn closure; *Duvet* for snap or nylon tape fastener closure; *Box-edge Cushion*, procedure #1 or #2, and *Knife-edge Pillow*, procedure #2 for zipper closures; *Pillow Shams* for a lapped closure.

CLOUD SHADE

See *Roman Shades*, procedure #11.

COMFORTER

Originally utilitarian bed coverings, comforters today are being used (with *pillow shams* and a *dust ruffle*) in place of bedspreads. This thick bedcover may have the *batting* stitched or tied in place. Make a top from large 8"–10" squares, a decorator fabric, a sheet, or any durable fabric. Make the bottom in matching or contrasting fabric that has the same cleaning requirements. Why not make a flannel comforter with a plaid top and a plain bottom and use the design of the plaid for knot placement or as a guide for stitching? For a custom touch, use *cording*, *ruffles*, or *trim* around the outer edges.

Use two or three layers of bonded polyester batting if thick comforter batting is not available. Cotton and wool batting tends to shift and needs knots placed 3"–4" apart and does not launder well; bonded polyester batting can have the knots 8"–10" apart and launders beautifully.

Use *Bed Measurements*, procedure #4 for a comforter or quilt without pillow covering to determine the measurements for a comforter, adding 3" extra to both the finished length and width measurement for *shrinkage* when the comforter is stitched or knotted and for seam allowances. Refer to *Bedspreads*, procedure #10 for Flat Floor-length and Coverlet Yardage Work Sheet and seam fabric widths together for the top and bottom, using procedure #11, rounding corners if desired.

Assemble Materials.

Prepare top and bottom as directed above. Purchase bonded polyester batting; thread for stitching; crochet cotton, pearl cotton, or polyester knitting worsted yarn and a large darning needle for knotting, and T-pins or extra long straight pins to hold batting in place. You will need a large area to work, preferably a room with wall-to-wall carpet or a large rug. For those without space to spread the comforter out on the floor, you can make a frame with four C-clamps (purchased at a hardware store), four 1" × 2" boards at least 12" longer than your fabric measurements, and a large quantity of push-pins. Make sure the frame is squared. Balance the frame on four chair backs or other furniture of nearly equal height when working.

Construction.

For the top fabric without a design to follow, make dots for knotting or as a guide for stitching, using a soft lead pencil. Mark at 8"–10" intervals, making a row down the center both lengthwise and crosswise; then fill in each quarter. Machine-baste trim, if being used, to the top edges.

When using carpet or rug, lay the batting on the floor, making sure each layer is smooth, if using more than one. Place top over batting, right side up, making fabric taut by inserting pins down into the carpet along all edges. Insert pins straight down into the carpet through the top and batting along the centers lengthwise and crosswise and then do each quarter. *Pin-baste* top to batting, removing pins from carpet as you work (A).

When using a frame, place the top fabric wrong side up and secure to frame with push-pins along the seam line at 12"–14" intervals. Place a sheet of batting over the top, making the batting smooth and wrinkle-free without stretching. Working from the underside of the frame, *pin-baste* batting to the top with long pins or use long, hand-sewn basting stitches. Pin-baste along the centers lengthwise and crosswise and then do each quarter. Pin batting to the top around the four edges as you remove the pushpins. Trim batting even with the top. Baste trim in place if being used (A).

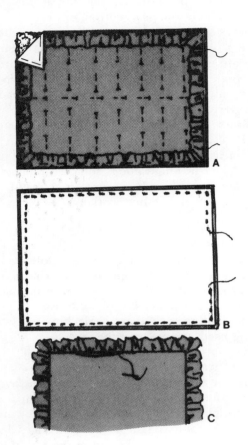

HINT: When making a king-size comforter, it may be necessary to pin the batting along all four edges, and then roll both the top and batting on each narrow end in order to reach the centers. With all four corners of the frame supported, remove the C-clamps from one end. Roll up fabric and batting on the board one-half the amount needed to reach the center of the comforter; reclamp boards together. Do the same for the opposite end. Pin-baste centers and quarters as required and then unroll to complete basting.

For either method, lay the bottom over the top, right sides together. Pin edges together through all thicknesses. Use a ⅝″ seam and start at least 12″ from the corner on the head end, stitch around the comforter through all thicknesses, leaving an opening for turning (B). *Trim* corners and trim excess batting close to stitching to reduce bulk. Turn right side out. Turn in opening edges ⅝″; pin together. Stitch opening shut by hand or machine (C).

When using carpet or rug, with top uppermost, spread comforter out smoothly on floor. Secure all edges by inserting pins into carpet, keeping all layers smooth. Insert pins through all layers, into the carpet, at marks or along the fabric design, repositioning previous pins as you work and keeping top and bottom wrinkle-free. Starting at one edge, slide hand under comforter at each pin. Swing pin around and pin-baste at each pin. This preliminary pinning will enable you to stitch or knot the layers together much more quickly.

When using a frame, with top uppermost, secure comforter to frame with pushpins along the seamed edges. Pin-baste all three layers together at marks, along fabric lines, or fabric designs, repositioning any previous pins as you work. Keep top and bottom wrinkle-free by sliding your hand under the comforter to guide the pin placement. This preliminary pinning will enable you to stitch or knot the layers much more quickly.

To stitch batting in place, follow the directions given for *Quilting by Machine.*

To knot, work on a table or other flat surface, making a knot at each pin mark. Thread darning needle with about 50″ of thread or yarn, making it double. Take ¼″ stitches at each pin. Insert needle ⅛″ from pin down through all thicknesses; reinsert needle and bring it back through the comforter on other side of pin. Pull thread until the end is about 2″ long (A).

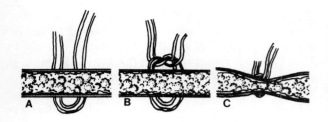

A   B   C

Tie into a square knot by lapping the short ends over the long threads with the needle. Tuck the short ends under the loop formed between the fabric and crossed threads (B). Pull knot up tight, pulling all layers of fabric and batting to form indentation on both sides of the comforter. To complete the knot, lap short ends under loop formed by the threads and pull knot tight. Cut threads to 1″ length above the knot (C).

COLOR

As one of the most important features of decorating, color is discussed thoroughly in the beginning of this book. Refer to the section called, "You, the Decorator," step 2.

COLOR HARMONY

Learn to analyze the components of each color you select. Because several basic colors are mixed together for most hues, you are choosing the "mix" as well as the color. For example, there may be several shades of plum among your fabric swatches, but one shade could have too much blue, red, or black in its dye and it would therefore clash with the rest of your color scheme.

COLOR INTENSITY

Any color can be made bright or dull. Retain the color, shade, or tint of the primary, secondary, or tertiary groups for a bright color that will reflect its intensity. Neutralize any of the three color groups by adding black to make them become a duller or less intense hue.

CORDED STRING HEM

A durable hem finish for *ruffles, tablecloths, napkins,* and *place mats.* A corded string hem works well for sheer, semisheer, light, or medium-weight fabric that is crisp and tightly woven and does not ravel easily. For cord, use a heavyweight crochet or pearl cotton that matches or contrasts and use thread the same color as the cord.

To make hem, use a medium-width zigzag stitch set at 20 stitches to the inch. Lay cord on right side of the fabric about ¼″ from the cut edge. Center cord under the presser foot, keeping the one edge of the foot close to the cut edge. Pull up cord through slot and hold lightly as you zigzag over it. Trim away excess fabric alongside the cord, being careful not to cut the stitches.

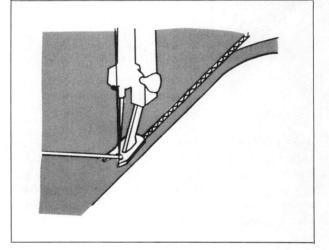

CORDING

A decorative edge that is made by covering a cord (specifically manufactured for this purpose) with self- or contrasting fabric. To make cording, use cord the desired thickness and *bias strips* or *straight-grain strips.* The strips should be wide enough to encircle the cord, plus 1″ for two ½″ seam allowances.

1. TO PREPARE CORDING, cut a piece of cord and a fabric strip as long as needed. Fold fabric wrong sides together over cord with long raw edges even. Using a zipper foot, *machine-baste* close to cord, but do not crowd the cord (A).

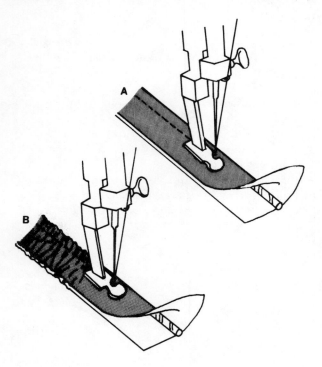

To make shirred cording, sometimes called ruching, prepare as above in step A, making the strip 1½ to 2 times as long as the cord. While basting strip around cord, stop with needle in fabric about every 6″; push fabric back along the cord, forming the shirred effect (B).

HINT: When preparing the cording, adjust zipper foot so the needle is at the innermost edge of the indentation. Baste cording in place along the original stitching, too. When stitching cording in a seam, adjust zipper foot so the needle is closer to the cording and the basting will not show on the right side when the seam is stitched.

---

2. CORDING FOR A HEM: Add a decorator touch to a floor-length *tablecloth,* a throw *bedspread,* or a *valance* with plump or narrow cording. To finish a hem edge, cut the strip wide enough to accommodate cord, plus 2″. Wrap strip around cord with 1½″ for a hem allowance and a ½″ seam allowance; pin and baste as in procedure #1, step A above (A).

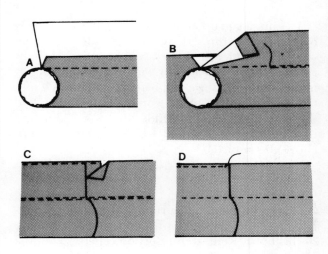

Turn in long wide hem edge ½″; press. Pin cording along edge to be hemmed with the seam allowance of the cording along the raw edge. Stitch in place, starting and ending 2″ from end of cord (B). Open stitching on cording and cut cords flush. Turn in fabric ½″ and lap over other end, making lap smooth, and complete stitching (C).

Turn cording down and hem allowance up to the inside, covering raw edges. Stitch hem in place by hand or machine, easing or stretching pressed edge to fit (D).

3. CORDING IN A SEAM: Sometimes called piping or welting, this classic seam finish may be made with *bias strips* or *straight-grain strips* and cord as tiny as 1/16″ or as plump as 1″ diameter. Use the size of cord that will best complement your decorating project. Prepare cording as instructed in procedure #1 above.

Using a zipper foot, place cording on the right side of one fabric section, *machine-baste* in place along the ½"–⅝" seam line, being careful not to crowd the cord (A).

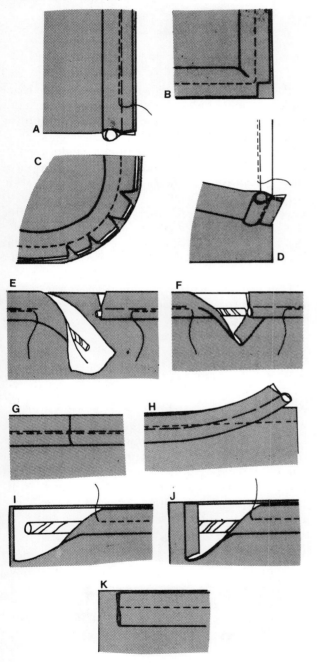

To turn cording at a corner or point, baste to within ½"–⅝" of next side. With needle in fabric, raise presser foot and clip cording fabric *only* to cording stitches. Pivot fabric on needle until next side is lined up with zipper foot; make sure cording seam allowances and fabric are flat. Drop presser foot and continue basting (B). For heavier fabrics or large cording, round the corner slightly.

For sharp curves or rounded corners, baste to within 1" of curve. Lay cording around curve, clipping cording seam allowances *only* as needed to make cording lie flat. Then continue basting (C).

To stitch the seam, place remaining section over basted cording section, with right sides together; pin. With the basting section uppermost, stitch seam to the left of the basting, crowding the cording slightly (D).

To make cording continuous, start at the center of one edge, leaving 1" of cording free. When the ends nearly meet, extend cording 1" over first end; cut off. Open this end of cording fabric; cut cord *only* so it is flush with the first end (E). Turn in fabric end ½", wrapping folded edge over cord at starting end, having cord ends meet (F). Baste remainder of cording in place, connecting with previous stitches (G).

To end cording at an intersecting seam that will not be corded, taper cording to nothing where it meets at the intersecting seam line (H).

To end cording at an edge, open cording fabric 1". Trim away ½"–⅝" of cord (I). Turn fabric over cord, making fabric flush with the intersecting seam or hem line, and then pull down the seam allowances over it (J). Machine-baste cording in place (K).

CORNICES

These decorative bands are used to conceal rods used to hang *curtains* and *draperies;* as toppers for the open-window look where shades (including *Roman shades*) are pulled up behind the cornice during the daytime. To use cornices to conserve energy, see *insulation.*

Cornices are usually 10″–12″ deep, but can be as wide as one-fifth the height measurement from floor to ceiling. The inside measurement should be 3″–5″ wider and longer than the curtains or draperies; for Roman shades extend 8″–10″ from wall to accommodate multilayered insulated lining, and make about 1″ longer.

1. BOX CORNICE. Use ½″-thick wood for the top, front, and two ends, cut to the inside measurements. Use wood glue on the intersecting edges and fasten the front to the ends with brads or finishing nails (A). Glue and nail the top in place (B).

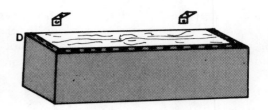

Pad the front and ends with batting or thin foam sheets. Staple or glue the padding in place, extending the edges to the inside and along the top for about 1″ (C).

Next place fabric over padding, centering any design. Wrap loosely, holding in place with push-pins. Cut away excess fabric, allowing enough fabric to just cover the padding. (It isn't necessary to cover the cornice top, unless it will be visible after the cornice is hung.) Staple or glue fabric to the inside lower edge, making corners smooth and flat; then wrap fabric smoothly over padding without flattening it. Cut away excess fabric (D).

Hang cornice with two or more *angle iron* brackets. *Anchor* to wall as required.

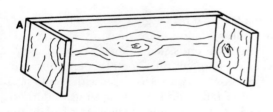

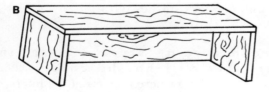

2. FLAT CORNICE. This style lends itself to corded edges. A flat cornice is often used to cover an entire wall to help make the window treatment a focal point. It can also be used in an alcove to frame the top of the window. Use ½″-thick wood the length of the wall or indentation, less ½″–1″ to allow for padding and fabric on the ends, and as deep as desired. Pad and cover flat cornice as directed for *Box Cornice,* steps A and B above. Hang flat cornice with three or more *angle iron* brackets. *Anchor* to wall or ceiling as required.

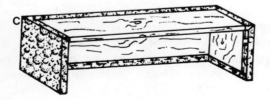

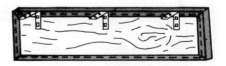

COUCH COVERS

Day beds, high-risers, and twin-size beds without a *headboard* often serve a dual purpose—a couch during the day and a bed at night in a studio apartment or to accommodate an overnight guest in a multifunction room. The styles are similar to those of *bedspreads* and only a slight change is needed to make them fit a couch. All four sides of the couch are covered, but the one long edge that is placed against the wall is made from a plain rectangle of fabric for the drop with a slit at each back corner.

1. FITTED BOX COUCH COVER.

Measure couch following *Bed Measurements,* procedure #2. You may want to review the suggestions in *Bedspread Fabric* and *Fabric Handling* to learn which fabrics are best for couch covers.

Determine yardage needed by using *Bedspreads,* procedure #2; Fitted Bedspread and Coverlet Yardage Work Sheet, adding 10″ extra to the drop circumference (6″ for ease, 4″ for four 1″ seam allowances to make slits). Cut out top. Cut out drop sections, piecing as necessary, making back drop section 4″ longer than measurement and making the front and side drop sections in one piece adding 6″. Stitch 1″ finished hems in place along the bottom of each drop section. To form slits, stitch drop sections together in a 1″ seam, starting ½″ from raw edge and ending 6″ away (A). Press seams open, turning in slit 1″. Turn in raw edges and stitch in place (B).

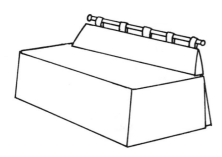

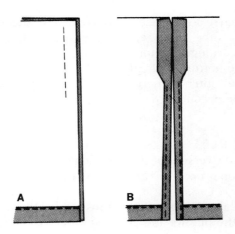

Pin drop to top, placing slits at the back corners, allowing 2″ extra at each long edge and 1″ extra at each end for easing. Distribute ease evenly; stitch drop in place. Turn right side out and shape corners. Place cover on couch and make a matching backrest following *headboard* suggestions or make *bolsters.*

2. FITTED BAND COUCH COVER.

Accent both edges of the band with self- or contrasting *cording* and make a pleated or gathered *drop.* The style shown has a gathered drop with a 6″ wide band. Subtract the band measurement from the drop measurement and add seam allowances to both long edges of the band.

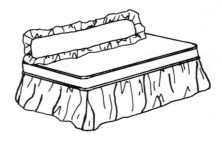

Follow the instructions for fitted box couch cover, above, and cut out band and back drop section using the same measurement as instructed for the box-shaped drop. Determine the fullness for a gathered drop or make a pattern for your pleats and calculate the yardage, using your requirements. Make cording, if being used, and baste to the top and the bottom long edge of the band. Hem drop sections; stitch gathered or pleated drop to band. Complete couch cover as in steps A, B, and C above.

COVERLET

A shorter version of the traditional *bedspread*. Construction procedures are explained throughout that category. *Comforters* are being used as coverlets as well. Make *pillow shams* for those styles that do not cover the pillows and add a *dust ruffle* to complete the look.

CRISP FABRICS

When selecting fabric you will need to know how it will drape. Crisp fabric will hang from a rod or seam in deep rounded folds, fanning outward at the free edge.

CROSSWISE

A term that refers to the threads that run across the fabric from selvage to selvage. This also refers to the crosswise grain of the fabric.

CURTAIN AND/OR DRAPERY RODS

The methods used for hanging curtains and stationary draperies have changed dramatically in the last few years. Two new stars are the 4½"-wide continental rod and a plastic plumbing pipe called PVC pipe.

The continental rod is being used to hang sheers, casement, hourglass, or sash curtains, all styles of stationary draperies, and valances (A).

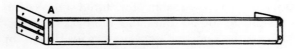

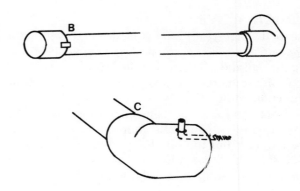

The PVC pipe is available in 1½"–6" diameter and has end caps or elbows that are at least ½" larger in diameter than the pipe (B). Printing on pipe requires them to be painted or covered with fabric when not covered by curtains or draperies. To install, use a 3" L-bend screw and drill a hole in the top of the pipe to insert the screw (C).

1. STANDARD CURTAIN RODS

come in two weights. Use the heavier ones to hang stationary draperies, heavyweight curtains, and valances. Pinch-pleated draperies and valances can be hung with the aid of pin hooks. Use single rods for sheers, tier curtains, or for a valance above casement, and sash curtains (A). Double rods are used to hang crisscross Priscilla curtains and sheers with stationary draperies or a valance (B).

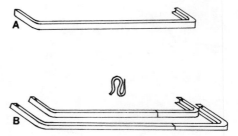

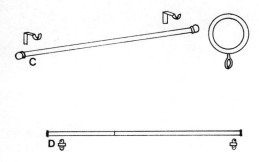

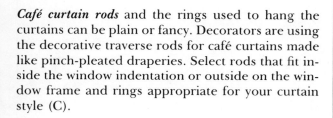

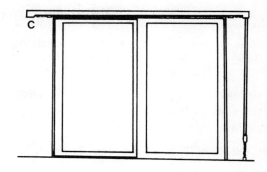

Café curtain rods and the rings used to hang the curtains can be plain or fancy. Decorators are using the decorative traverse rods for café curtains made like pinch-pleated draperies. Select rods that fit inside the window indentation or outside on the window frame and rings appropriate for your curtain style (C).

Sash and door curtain rods are used for casement, hourglass, and sash curtains of sheer or lightweight fabric and are hung next to the glass (D).

2. DRAPERY TRAVERSE RODS are made so you can open and close your drapes. They can be found in many combinations. These rods may be decorative with the rod above the drape (A) or be covered by the draperies when closed (B).

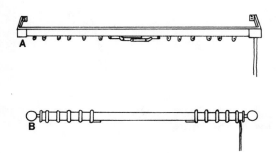

You may select traverse rods with a flat curtain rod to hang draw drapes and sheer curtains. Double traverse rods may be used for several different treatments so the glass can be exposed, covered with one set of drapes, or both. Combine lined drapes with sheer drapes or open-weave unlined drapes on the front rod with lined drapes next to the glass for direct or infused light. In extremely cold climates, you may use classic lined drapes on the front rod with a special insulated lining drape on the rod next to the glass. Double and single traverse rods also come with valance rods. They may have center or left and right openings for corner windows and sliding glass doors.

When using traverse rods on windows and sliding glass doors, an allowance must be made for stacking the drapery folds so they will clear the opening when the drapes are pulled open. Add one-third of the window width to the rod to allow the draperies to stack back off the window (C).

HINT: Use wall hooks for traverse rods that are covered when the draperies are closed, and ceiling hooks for decorative rods.

Be sure to measure your windows accurately as directed in *Measuring Windows.*

To determine the number of fabric widths needed for each window, the following calculations are needed:

Window width _____

Plus stacking (if any, see step C above)   + _____

Equals finished width   = _____

Times fullness (this includes seam and side hems) 2½, 3, 3½ × _____ = _____

Plus returns and/or overlap measurements   + _____

Equals total cut width   = _____

Divide by fabric width 36", 44", 48", 54", 60"   ÷ _____

Equals number of fabric widths   = _____

To determine the cut length for curtains or draperies the following calculations are needed, including the Casing, Heading, **and** Hem **requirements as indicated for each style of** Curtain **or** Draperies:

Finished length _____

Plus casing or heading   + _____

Plus hem   + _____

Equals cut length   = _____
    For fabric with pattern repeat
    Divide cut length by *pattern repeat* length   ÷ _____

    Equals number of repeats per length. If fraction remains, round up to next full
       number.   = _____

    Multiply by length of repeat   × _____

    Equals adjusted cut length   = _____

Actual cut-length measurement _____

Times the number of fabric widths   × _____

Equals yardage in inches   = _____

Divided by 36   ÷ 36

Equals total yardage required for one pair of Curtains or Draperies   = _____

Lining Yardage Requirement

Use total cut width measurement		_____
Less 6" not needed for side hems	−	6
Equals adjusted cut lining width	=	_____
Divide by width of lining 48", 54"	÷	_____
Equals number of lining widths	=	_____
Cut-length measurement		_____
Times number of lining widths	×	_____
Equals yardage in inches	=	_____
Divided by 36	÷	36
Equals total yardage required for one pair of draperies	=	_____

CURTAINS

Make an elegant window treatment as your first decorating project with these straight-line beauties. Let your fabric tell the story. Select easy-to-handle sheers, light- to medium-weight fabrics with an elegant design, or a sheet. No matter what fabric you choose, the construction is easy. Remember that each pair of curtains consists of two completed panels that are made to the required fullness before they are gathered on a rod or hung on the rod with rings.

Move on to *Café, Casement,* and *Hourglass Curtains* found in this section to add variety, or include tiebacks, explained in *Tieback Curtains and Draperies.*

After you have selected the style curtain you want to make, it is wise to purchase and install the curtain rod (see *Curtain and/or Drapery Rods*). Next, measure the window(s) accurately, following instructions in *Measuring Windows.* Using the measurements, turn

HINT: When using sheets, purchase the size that will work best for your measurements. Be aware that it is almost impossible to match large *pattern repeats* when using more than one sheet. Sheets can create the same problem when you have more than one window in your room.

back to the *Curtain and/or Drapery Yardage Work Sheet* to determine the amount of fabric to purchase. To help evaluate the quality of fabric you may purchase, see *Fabric Handling.*

Do not pull a thread to straighten fabric ends when cutting out each panel. To straighten solid-colored fabric, see *Straightening Fabric Ends;* for fabric with a design, see *Pattern Repeats,* procedure #3.

When stitching fabric widths is necessary, trim away selvages and stitch seam. *Clean-finish* seam allowances with a mock French seam, step E for sheers.

1. STRAIGHT CURTAINS.

This style of curtain has a *casing* with or without a heading that is used to hang it on the rod and doubled hems on the remaining edges.

Style requirements.

For side hems, allow 6″ for two doubled 1½″ hems (3″ for each side) and 6″ for the bottom hem to make a 3″ doubled hem for each panel. To finish the top, see *Casing,* procedure #1 for a plain casing to be used when the curtain top will be totally covered by stationary *draperies, cornice, lambrequin, swag,* or *valance* and procedure #2 for a casing with a heading if your curtain will be used alone.

To make each panel, stitch fabric widths together, if required. Make side hems first. Turn in side edges 3″, wrong sides together; press. Turn in raw edges to meet fold; press hem flat; pin. To hold hems in place, stitch close to inner fold (A). To *blind-stitch* hems in place, see *Hems.* Make bottom hem in the same manner, turning up the edge 6″ and then folding in the raw edge to meet the fold. When pinning hem in place, make sure the ends do not show on the right side of the panel (B). Complete curtain top with a casing.

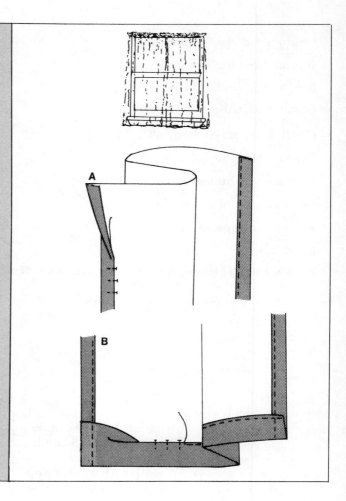

HINT: This style of curtain may be hung so the panels meet at the center or frame each side of the window and can be tied back with ribbons, cords with tassels, or self-fabric *tiebacks.*

2. CAFE CURTAINS.

Originally used in a café to cover the bottom half of the of the window for privacy, these simple curtains were held in place with rings that slid along a horizontal bar. Any fabric may be used, from sheer to medium-heavyweight. Today's decorators use café curtains in a full-length treatment composed of two or three tiers or with other window treatments for privacy in the most formal or casual room. You can make the tops plain, scalloped, or pleated and add your own touch to frame them for spectacular looking windows.

Quick flat cafe curtains. This style has a plain, smooth top that ripples from back to front between the rings. Be sure to review the measuring and yardage information at the beginning of this *Curtain* section.

Style requirements: Café curtains hang from rings. To find the finished length, measure from the bottom of the ring to the sill or to the bottom edge of the apron. For all types of fabric, add 6″ to the width measurement for two 1½″ doubled hems. To the length measurement add 3″ for a 1½″ doubled hem; for headings, add 8″ to accommodate a 4″-wide stiffening (purchase enough to stiffen the top of each panel between the side hems).

To make each panel, the side and bottom hems are pressed in place first, but not stitched until after the stiffening is applied. Turn in the side and bottom edges 3″; press. Turn in the side raw edges to meet fold; press and pin only. Open out side hems at the top and place the stiffening along the cut edge between the outer hem creases. Stitch ¼″ from both edges of stiffening (A). Pin and stitch side hems in place, then do the bottom hem, making sure the ends do not show on the right side of the panel (B). To make heading, turn down the top along the stiffening; press. Turn it down again along the other stiffening edge; press and stitch the heading in place (C).

Clip or sew on rings at even intervals, placing one at each end near the side edges. Thread rod through rings. Curtains will hang in soft rolling folds from the rod (D).

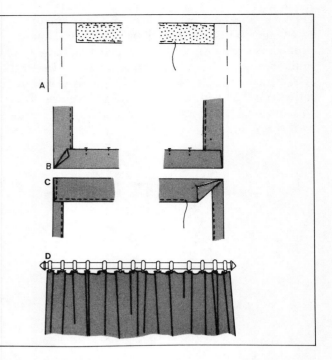

For a more contained look, form pleats on each panel held in place with clip rings. Divide the excess width into about 2″ sections for 1″ deep pleats, making spaces between pleats equal. Start and end about 3″ from each side edge; press pleat folds flat across the heading. Hold pleats together by placing the double prong in front and the single prong in back (E).

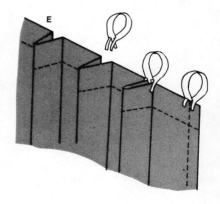

Other styles may be made, such as a café length, with tabs instead of rings (see *Draperies,* procedures #7 and #9), or make formal lined or unlined draperies as discussed in *Draperies.* Use the classic pinch pleat lined style and hang from a decorative traverse rod, or make the unlined version with pleater tape and café curtain pleater hooks with rings (F).

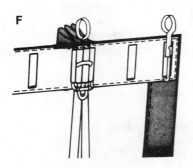

3. CASEMENT CURTAINS.

Originally, casement curtains were used only on windows and doors that are hung upright at the side edges. Casement curtains are currently being used with other window treatments on the lower half of any window for privacy. This style of curtain is secured with a rod at the top and bottom of the curtain for both doors and windows. Use sheer or open-weave fabric for the best results. You may be able to pull a thread on some sheers to straighten the ends. If you cannot, see *Straightening Fabric Ends.* Be sure to review the measuring and yardage information at the beginning of this *Curtain* section.

Casement curtains have a *casing* with a heading at the top and bottom in order to hold it flat against the glass with two rods. Note: Hang the rods after the curtain has been made, or measure an existing curtain. Make one continuous panel for each window, French door, or windowed entrance door with narrow side hems, piecing if necessary.

Style requirements: For casement windows, French doors, entrance doors, or sash windows, allow enough fabric, between the casings, to cover the glass so the casings do not show from the outside. Use the *Curtain and/or Drapery Yardage Work Sheet,* filling in the appropriate measurements to determine the amount of fabric needed.

To determine the cut width for the casement curtain panel, use your finished width measurement, multiplied by one of the suggested fullnesses on the work sheet. To determine the finished length, add the following measurements to your glass length measurement when using the standard sash or door curtain rod. For wider curtain rods or a different size heading, these allowances must be adjusted. To the glass measurement, add 5″ (1″ for two ½″ headings, 3″ for two 1½″ casings so the finished casings will be above the glass at the top and bottom of the window, and 1″ for *shrinkage* when the curtain is gathered on the rods and installed). To determine the actual cut length for the panel, add another 5″ to the established finished length measurement to finish the wrong side of the panel, using 2½″ to finish the top casing and 2½″ to finish the bottom casing (½″ for each heading, 2″ for each casing that will be finished 1½″ wide).

To make casement curtain, cut fabric panel as determined, seaming any fabric widths together. Make side hems first. Turn in side edges 1″, wrong sides together; press. Turn in raw edges to meet fold; press. Stitch inner folds of side hems in place (A). Make the *casing* with a heading, procedure #2, at top and bottom of curtain (B).

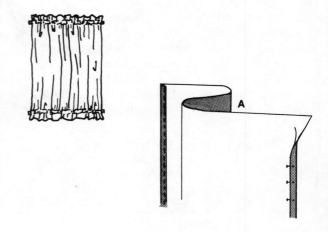

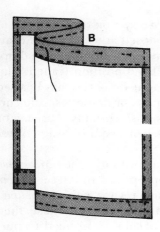

4. HOURGLASS CURTAINS: Sewn exactly like the *casement curtains* above, hourglass curtains need a slight adjustment so the side hems arch gracefully when tied at the center. To determine the length, use the glass length plus 9," then add an additional 2" for every 12" of the glass length. To test, pin fabric to curtain rods to see how much longer the side hems need to be, allowing ½ to ⅓ of the window to be covered where it will be tied to form the hourglass look.

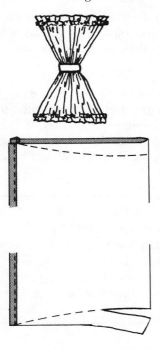

To shape the top and bottom hems, divide the fabric into thirds lengthwise. The center third should be the same length recommended for the casement curtain above. Divide the extra length equally between the top and bottom edges; trim away the flat area, tapering both sides to the established length for the side hems.

Make side hems first and then make the casings at the top and bottom, easing and stretching the casing to fit (the puckers and pleats will be lost in the folds when the curtain is hung). Hang curtain and tie a ribbon around the center to achieve the hourglass effect.

CUSHIONS

Designed to sit on, kneel on, lean against, or lie on, cushions are constructed of feathers, foam, or polyester fiberfill. Sometimes they have springs and horsehair padding and are covered with a decorator fabric or leather. Cushions may be from 1" to 6" thick and are usually quite tailored. See *Bolsters,* Round, Bonbon, and Wedge; *Box-edge Cushions:* Classic cover with cording, Quick Box-edge cushion covers, Turkish-corner Box-edge cushion covers; *Chair Cushions:* Tie-on, Reupholstered Chair Seats.

DAYBED COVERS

See *Couch Covers* for construction; *Bolsters* and *Headboards* for backrests.

DECORATIVE FINISHES

See *Bias Binding, Corded String Hem, Hems, Ruffles,* and *Trims.*

DECORATIVE SEAMS

See *Cording*, procedure #2, *Ruffles*, procedure #5, and *Trims*, procedure #3

DESIGN REPEATS

See *Pattern Repeats.*

DOORS

Doors present a challenge to the do-it-yourself decorator. They not only let light in, but also need to be covered for privacy. French doors, windowed entrance doors, and sliding glass doors, all require thought and individuality when decorated to enhance the total look of your room.

French doors may open inward or outward; make *curtains, draperies, roller shades,* or *Roman shades* that do not interfere with the doors as you enter or exit. Windowed entrance doors need to be covered in such a way to ensure privacy and allow you to screen visitors. Select extra-full sheers or lightweight fabrics when making casement or hourglass curtains for French or windowed doors.

Sliding glass doors need window treatments that will clear the section that will open when it is being used. Create a wall of glass by day and use a cover-up for nighttime as an energy saver and for privacy. Use both fabric and lining to prevent heat loss in cold weather and to help keep the house cooler in warm weather.

DOUBLE RUFFLES

See *Ruffles*, procedures #1 and #2 for a hem finish; procedures #1 and #4 for a decorative finish.

DRAPERIES

For your first drapery project, use an easy-to-sew fabric that does not require matching the design. Use plain dyed decorator fabrics, polished cotton, denim, lightweight corduroy, a fabric with an all-over small design, sheets, or even a more luxurious fabric such as rocket satin that is easy to handle.

Draperies are hung in two ways: on traverse rods so they can be opened or closed at will (called "draw draperies") or on unmovable rods where the draperies are arranged in a fixed position (called "stationary draperies"). Opaque draperies may be used alone or with sheer curtains or draperies, café curtains, casement curtains, sash curtains, Austrian or Roman shades, cornices, lambrequins, swags, or valances.

Carefully measure your windows (see *Measuring Windows*), select an appropriate rod (see *Curtain and/or Drapery Rods*), and review *Fabric Handling.* Choose the style of drapery you want to make, then determine the amount of fabric you need to purchase (see *Curtain and/or Drapery Yardage Work Sheet*).

1. DRAW DRAPERY STYLE REQUIREMENTS. This style of drapery always has a pleated heading and may be lined or unlined.

For side hems, allow 6″ for two 3″ hem allowances to make 1½″-wide doubled hems. For the *bottom hem* allow 8″ for a 4″-wide doubled hem.

For an unlined drapery heading, allow ½″ for pleater tape; 4½″ for opaque fabric; and 8″ for sheer fabric to accommodate a 4″-wide stiffening.

For a lined drapery heading, allow ½″ for the heading and use 4″-wide stiffening. Lining fabrics requirements may vary if the lining width is narrower than the fabric. Lining is cut 6″ narrower than the drapery cut width and is 1″ shorter in length.

HINT: In some hot countries, a lining is made exactly like the drape in width and 1″ shorter. Place the two layers wrong sides together, with top and side edges even; finish top with pleater tape and secure side edges together with a 1″ long thread anchor near hems and at several other spots.

---

2. QUICK UNLINED DRAW DRAPERIES WITH A PLEATER TAPE HEADING. Cut as many fabric lengths as needed. Stitch fabric widths together as required for wide windows. Trim seam allowances to ¼" and zigzag as explained in *Clean-finish* as selvages may cause the seam to pucker.

Turn in long side edges 3", wrong sides together; press. Turn in raw edges to meet fold; press and pin. Stitch close to inner fold to hold hem in place (A). Turn up bottom edge 8"; press. Turn in raw edge to meet fold; press and pin, making sure the ends won't show on the right side of the drapery. Stitch hem in place (B).

To make heading, on the right side, lap top of pleater tape ½" over raw edge of drapery panel (with hook pocket opening edge free). Line up one pocket with each side hem, turning in the tape end close to the pocket; pin. If there is a little excess tape, make tiny pleats between the pockets. Stitch top edge to panel (C). Turn tape to the inside along the stitched edge; press. Pin in place so the ends won't show on the right side of the panel. Stitch along ends and across remaining long edge of tape (D). Insert pleater hooks into pockets, forming pleats (E).

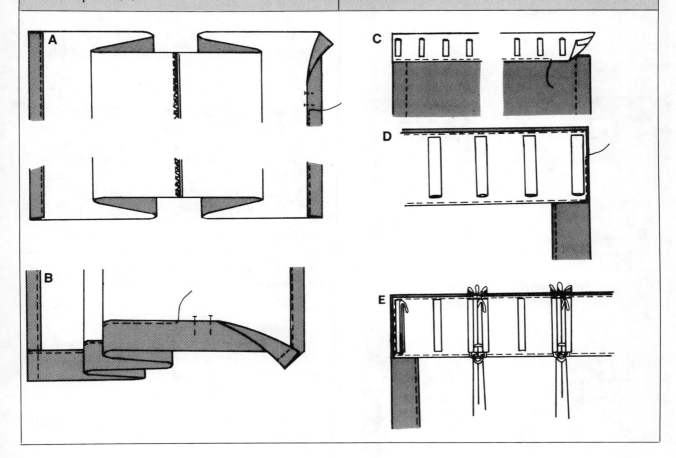

3. CLASSIC UNLINED DRAW DRAPERIES.

This method may be used for either opaque or sheer fabric. Use for opaque fabrics when your windows do not get a lot of direct sunlight, or when they are protected by blinds, shades, sheer curtains, or sheer draperies.

Cut as many lengths as needed. Stitch fabric widths together for wide windows and *clean-finish* seams with steps D or E. Turn in and press and pin long side hems and bottom hem as in procedure #2, steps A and B above, but *do not* stitch hems in place at this time.

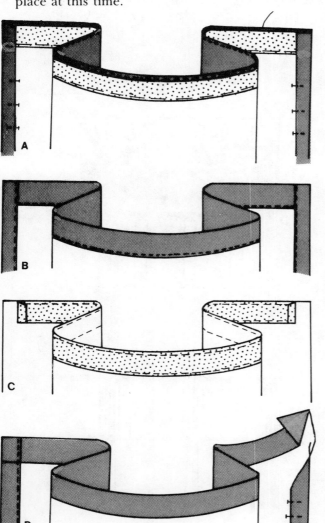

To make heading, open out side hems at the top of the panel. For *opaque fabrics,* place stiffening ½" from raw edge between the side hem creases, allowing a 1" turnback at each end of stiffening. Stitch ¼" from inner edge. Turn raw edge over remaining stiffening edge; stitch in place through all thicknesses (A). Turn down along upper stiffening edge; press (B). For *sheer fabrics,* place stiffening along upper raw edge between the side hem creases, allowing a 1" turnback at end of the stiffening. Stitch ¼" from upper edge (C). Turn down top edge along stiffening; press. Turn down again, enclosing stiffening; press (D).

For both styles of heading, stitch side and bottom hems in place as directed for procedure #2, steps A and B above. For a custom finish, *blind-stitch* hems in place by hand or machine. Make pleats in heading as directed below.

4. SELF-PLEATED HEADINGS.

The heading of each panel must be reduced in width to fit the rod, with a little slack, and represents one-half your finished width measurement. Make provisions for returns and overlaps for regular traverse rods or for overlaps for decorative rods. Allow 2"–4" (if you do not have the rods) at each side of the panel before making the first pleat or make the space as wide as the return on one side and at the inner edge of the overlapping bar at the opening edge. Mark these two places with pins. Use up excess heading width, allowing 4"–5" for each pleat and 2½"–4½" for spaces between pleats.

Make a tuck for each pleat. Pin a tuck at the return and opening spaces, taking fabric on the inside of each pin. Fold panel in half, matching end tucks, and pin another tuck of equal depth at the center (A). Divide the remaining two spaces into an equal number of tucks and spaces, making all spaces the same width (B).

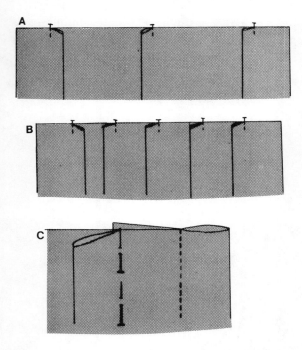

the bottom along the inner stiffening edge or sew the folds securely by hand (B). Pleats will stand up crisply (C).

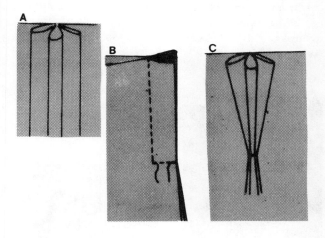

Mark and pin the remaining panel and then place the panels wrong sides together, making sure the return spaces fall together for the left and right side of the window with any narrower opening spaces at the center. Pin pleat tucks with another pin at each edge of the stiffening, making sure that the two pins point toward the top. Keep folds straight with vertical lines parallel and perpendicular to the top. To stitch pleat tucks, start at the right edge. Turn side edge under panel and make pleat fold flat, keeping top edges of pleat tuck and spaces even. Stitch $1/32''$– $1/16''$ inside the pin markings to allow for "shrinkage," since fabric weight and tension of the pleat stitching will reduce the total width when all pleats are stitched and shaped. *Back-stitch* at the beginning and end, removing pins as you work. End at the inner end of stiffening (C).

To make pinch-pleats, divide the large pleat tuck into three small pleats of equal size. Flatten side pleats against the stitching, then pull up the center to form a third pleat with the inner folds close to the stitching (A). Bring pleats together at this point. Pinch fabric tight and press. Stitch across

To make box pleats, divide the large pleat tuck in half over the stitching; press lightly (A). Sew invisibly to panel at upper corners and at the inner edge of stitching (B).

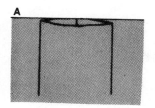

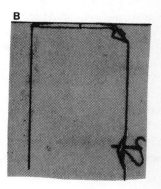

To make cartridge pleats, shape pleat tuck into a rounded shape. They may need to be stuffed or stiffened with a roll of heavy paper or cardboard. The heading may be divided into single tucks the same as pinch or box pleats (A), or in groups of three (B), or use narrow spaces and tucks (see *Pleats*).

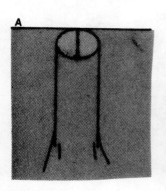

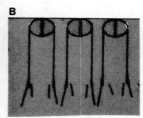

5. LINED DRAW DRAPERIES.

Lined draperies are as easy to make as unlined styles and the look is more professional. Lining can also act as an insulator and protect the drapery fabric from fading. Follow measuring, yardage instructions, and procedure #1 at the beginning of this *Draperies* section.

Straighten drapery and lining fabric ends. Cut as many drapery and lining panels as you need. Join drapery fabric seams needed for extra wide panels, matching *pattern repeats;* press seams open. Raw edges do not need to be finished when covered with lining. Stitch lining fabric widths together; press seams open.

With right sides together and upper edges even, pin lining to drapery panel along one long edge. Stitch in a 1½" seam, ending 10" above the bottom edge of the lining (A). Bring lining to opposite side. Pin and stitch remaining long edges together in the same manner (B). Press seam allowances toward

drapery along the stitching. Center lining over drapery panel; pin. Stitch upper edges together in a ½" seam (C).

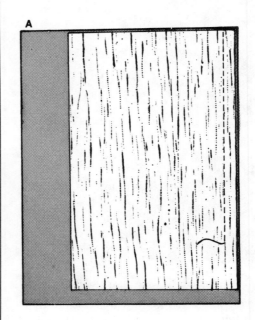

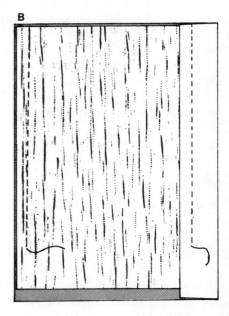

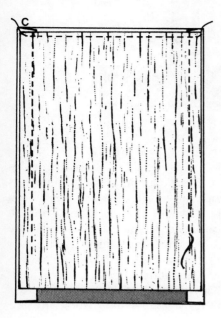

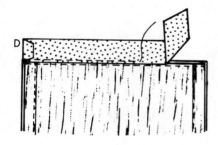

For a self-pleated heading (see procedure #4 above), cut a strip of stiffening the length of the upper edge of the panel, plus 2". Lap over top seam allowances with long edge of stiffening along seam stitching, turning back 1" at each end. Stitch to seam allowance (D). Turn drapery and lining right side out. Press top and side edges, making sure lining does not show on the right side at the top (E). The seam allowances of the lining and drapery fabric should lie along the fold of the side hem edges and act as a stiffening so the side edges do not curl.

For a pleater tape heading, prepare the panel as in steps A through E, eliminating the stiffening. Place pleater tape at top of panel over the lining with hook pocket opening pointed toward the hem edge. Line up one pocket at each side edge, turning in the ends ½"; pin. (See procedure #2, step D above.) If there is a little excess tape, make tiny pleats on both edges between the pockets. Stitch tape in place along all edges, through all thicknesses.

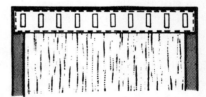

To hem, turn up lower edges of drapery and lining fabrics 8"; press. Turn in raw edges to meet folds; press and pin. Stitch drapery and lining hems in place (A). *Blind-stitch* drapery and lining hems in place for a custom touch. Complete side hem stitching (B). Turn seam allowances toward side hem. *Slip-stitch* lower end and side of draperies to the hem, catching only one layer of the hem so the stitches do not show on the right side of the panel (C).

HINT: Finish heading before hemming the bottom, if you need to adjust the length for uneven floors.

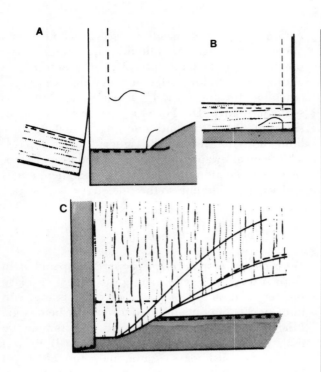

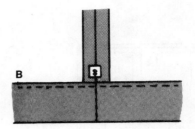

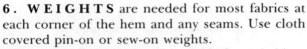

6. WEIGHTS are needed for most fabrics at each corner of the hem and any seams. Use cloth covered pin-on or sew-on weights.

After pressing hem in place and before stitching, open out the hem layers. Pin or tack weight to side hem seam allowance just above the hem crease (A). Complete hem as explained in procedure #5 above. Pin or tack weight to the seam allowance only to make the seam hang in a straight line (B).

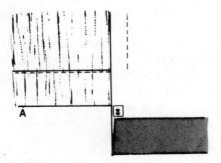

7. STATIONARY DRAPERY

STYLE requirements are as varied as the styles you may choose. They may be made as simply as *curtains,* using opaque fabric, that are hung on a standard curtain rod and tied back with ribbon; hung on a decorator rod that has been covered with matching fabric, or painted and hung at each side of the window. Or a valance may be inserted between the two panels and then tied back or let hang free. PVC pipes and continental rods will give your stationary draperies a high-fashion look. Review *Curtain and/or Drapery Yardage Work Sheet, Curtains* and *Tieback Curtains and Draperies* to make your own stationary draperies an original creation. See *Rod Covers* to cover a rod with matching fabric.

Stationary draperies used over sheer curtains or mini-blinds may not need a lining as these additional window coverings will help protect the draperies from the sun. There are two ways to line stationary draperies: the traditional way, with a 1½″ hem on the underside, or with the lining at the edge.

For the traditional method, unlined or lined, follow procedure #1 at the beginning of this section to estimate the fabric and lining yardage; procedures #2 and #3 for unlined styles; and procedure #5 for a lined version. For headings, use a *casing* with or without a heading or the self-pleated headings explained in procedure #4. For casings on thick round or wide flat rods, measure from the floor to the bottom of the rod; add circumference of rod at thickest part (doubling the amount for the heading if used), plus ½″ for turnunder and about 1″ for *shrinkage* as long, lined draperies gathered on a rod will fan out at the hem edge making it shorter.

Update a bathroom with a sink skirt and shower curtain with a matching valance, all done in one pattern with fabric and wallcovering by Waverly Fabrics. See *Bathrooms,* procedures #1 and #2, and *Valances.*

An informal conversation area is decorated with coordinated fabrics from Waverly Fabrics' Highland Collection. Box-edge cushions and wedge-shaped bolsters enhance platforms covered with matching fabric, while the decorator pillows add contrast. See *Box-edge Cushions,* procedures #1 and #2; *Bolsters,* procedure #3; and *Knife-edge Pillows,* procedures #1, #2, and #5.

An unusually handsome bedroom was brought about with Waverly Fabrics' striped Alouette and moiré taffeta fabrics. The bed's coverlet with dust ruffle and slipcovered headboard is surrounded by a canopy that is made like the lined-to-edge draperies and corded valance at the window. To carry out this pleasing look, a flat Roman shade, a floor-length tablecloth, throw pillows, and a matching upholstered chair are included. See *Bedspreads,* procedures #9 through #12; *Canopy; Cording; Curtains,* procedure #1; *Draperies,* procedures #7 and #8; *Knife-edge Pillows; Roman Shades,* procedures #1 through #6; *Tablecloths; Tieback Curtains and Draperies;* and *Valances.*

Add pizzazz to a dining room with Waverly Fabrics' Country Collection. The café curtains and place mats are made from Baxter Stripe and the chair cushions from Baxter. See *Chair Cushions,* procedure #1; *Curtains,* procedure #2; and *Napkins, Place Mats, and Table Runners.*

A quiet spot in your dining area can be enclosed in sash curtains with matching valances and seat cushions. Add a table runner and chair cushions that match the wallcovering and trim the pillows with cording and bands cut from the striped fabric. Both fabric and wallcoverings are from Waverly Fabrics. See *Box-edge Cushions,* procedure #1; *Chair Cushions,* procedure #1; *Cording; Curtains,* procedure #1; *Napkins, Place Mats, and Table Runners;* and *Valances.*

This gathered slipcover in a tie-on throw style with nonsewn cushions was done in a decorator fabric from Calico Corners at Denver, Colorado, to complement the two-tier café curtains with pinch-pleated headings. See *Curtains,* procedure #2; *Draperies,* procedures #4 and #5; *Knife-edge Pillows,* procedure #5; and *Slipcovers.*

A windowseat in this child's room is a perfect spot for day-dreaming. The casement curtains, a thick, box-edge cushion with shirred cording, nonsewn pillows, and upholstered walls use fabric from Waverly Fabrics. See *Box-edge Cushions,* procedure #1; *Cording; Curtains,* procedure #3; *Knife-edge Pillows,* procedure #5; and *Walls,* procedures #1, #2, and #3.

This formal dining room was decorated with fabrics from Waverly Fabrics' French Collection. The shirred canopied ceiling is draped with Charmant; the draperies with flat cornices, covering the sheer curtains, are made with Delice (both fabrics have a light-colored background). The table runners and napkins are Mignon in green, and the reupholstered chair seats are Amical in rust. See *Chair Cushions,* procedure #3; *Cornices,* procedure #2; *Curtains,* procedure #1; *Draperies,* procedure #7; *Napkins, Place Mats, and Table Runners;* and *Tieback Curtains and Draperies.*

Above: A quiet corner to relax with privacy has three-quarter-length draperies with tab hangers, an upholstered couch, and pillows with cording and harem corners. All are made in color-coordinated fabrics from Waverly Fabrics. See *Draperies,* procedure #9; and *Knife-edge Pillows,* procedures #1, #2, and #4.

Above: A nursery with classic draw draperies in fabric from Calico Corners in Denver, Colorado, has the same panda bear appliqué on the patchwork comforter, quilted chair pads, and floor pillow. See *Comforters; Cording; Draperies,* procedures #4 and #5; *Knife-edge Pillows;* and *Quilting by Machine.*

Left: Relax in elegance and comfort in a room that features fabric by Jay Yang for Fabriyaz. The lambrequin, with a flat, unlined Roman shade underneath, is covered with the same fabric as the upholstered couches. Turkish-cornered cushions and harem-cornered pillows add a splash of color along with the tablecloth seen through the window. See *Box-edge Cushions,* procedure #3; *Knife-edge Pillows,* procedure #4; *Lambrequin;* and *Tablecloths.*

Sumptuous fabric by Jay Yang for Fabriyaz enhances the stationary tieback draperies, couch cushion, round bolster with sunburst ends, and flanged pillows that are coordinated with the wallcovering by Jay Yang for Carefree. See *Bolsters,* procedure #1; *Box-edge Cushions,* procedure #1; *Draperies,* procedure #7; *Knife-edge Pillows,* procedures #3 and #6; and *Tieback Curtains and Draperies.*

The magnificence of a decorator fabric by Jay Yang for Fabriyaz has been used in two classic ways that are perfect for this traditional bedroom. The coverlet-length, corded, fitted box bedspread is quilted along the fabric's design and the floor-to-ceiling draperies are lined-to-edge with the same solid colored fabric that is used for the dust ruffle. See *Bedspreads,* procedures #1 through #4; *Cording; Draperies,* procedures #4, #5, and #8; and *Dust Ruffle,* procedure #1.

Above: Sheets in a juvenile print are an excellent choice to make a flat Roman shade with a multilayered insulated lining and a matching box cornice for a child's room that is energy efficient. See *Cornices*, procedure #1, and *Roman Shades*, procedures #1 through #5.

Above: A throw-style slipcovered chair in a folded, pinned, and tie-on style was draped in decorator fabric from Calico Corners in Denver, Colorado, using the same fabric for nonsewn pillows on the floor for relaxing in front of the fireplace. See *Knife-edge Pillows*, procedure #5, and *Slipcovers*.

Above: For a bright sunroom that is used year-round, quick seasonal changes can be made with fabric from Waverly Fabrics. The wicker chair has corded cushions with a matching knife-edge pillow, accented with an eyelet ruffle. The round table has a floor-length tablecloth and a three-quarter-length topper, each trimmed with an applied, contrasting ruffle with a heading. See *Box-edge Cushions*, procedure #1; *Cording*; *Knife-edge Pillows*; *Ruffles*; and *Tablecloths*.

Waverly Fabrics' French Collection is used again in this bedroom. The shirred wallcovering with pleats under the window was done in Mignon and the draperies and dressing table in Charmant, both in the same light background. The stool and chair are upholstered in rust-colored Amical. See *Draperies,* procedure #7; *Tablecloths; Tieback Curtains and Draperies;* and *Walls,* procedures #1, #2, and #5.

Create an unusual sitting room that invites guests to tarry, with an abundance of cushions and pillows, and draperies in coordinating fabric from Waverly Fabrics. The wicker settee has a striped floral box-edge cushion and knife-edge pillows, plus accents of solid-color textured fabric pillows and floral pillows that match the stationary tieback draperies. The side chairs have textured solid-color box-edge cushions with contrasting pillows. An oversized upholstered ottoman in the striped print gives balance to this elegantly simple room. See *Box-edge Cushions,* procedures #2 and #3; *Draperies,* procedure #7, and *Knife-edge Pillows,* procedure #1.

8. LINED-TO-EDGE DRAPERIES.

Sometimes called handkerchief draperies because of the flat construction, this style requires a contrast fabric of equal weight to the decorator fabric. Tie or pin back the draperies to show the contrast side. With this type of lining, you may stitch the lining to the decorator fabric along all four edges of each panel or you may stitch the side and top edges together and have the bottom edge open and finished with the traditional 4″ doubled hem.

Ruffles and/or *cording* used along the front and hem edges add a custom touch. Tab hangers or rings such as those used for café curtains (see *Curtains,* procedure #2) are sometimes used on plain, flat-style stationary draperies without pleats or gathers. The extra fullness is arranged on the rod so the fabric ripples in and out between the hangers.

After drapery yardage is calculated using procedure #1 above, use the same amount for lining or contrast fabric.

To construct the stitched hem style, place the two sections right sides together, with all edges even; pin. Starting and ending on the top edge, stitch edges together in a ½″–⅝″ seam, leaving an opening for turning (A). Press seams open as far as possible.

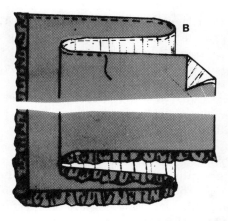

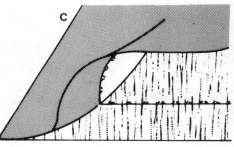

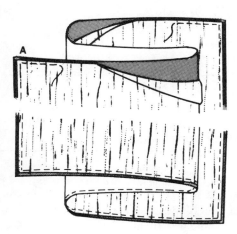

Turn panel right side out. Press all edges flat, turning in the opening along the established seam line; stitch opening edges shut(B). Complete heading as planned.

To construct the open hem style, place the two sections right sides together, with all edges even; pin. Stitch side and top edges in a ½″–⅝″ seam. Press seams open and turn panel right side out. Press side and top edges flat.

Make bottom hems by turning up both the drapery and lining 8″; press. Turn in raw edges to meet fold; press and pin. Stitch hems in place (C).

9. TAB HANGER STATIONARY DRAPERIES with box pleats are hung from decorative rods with tabs long enough to accommodate their thickness. Made of self-fabric or *band trim,* tab hangers are usually more economical than purchased rings. This is an excellent style for café curtains as well.

Calculate yardage as for Classic Unlined Draw Draperies procedure #3, using a ½″ heading allowance. Additional fabric is needed for a 5″-wide facing strip as long as the finished width measurement, and for at least 14 tabs for each pair of draperies 5″ wide and 7″–11″ long to accommodate the rod. Wider drapes will require more tabs. Use 4″-wide stiffening the length of the facing.

Make box pleats following procedure #4 in the Draw Drapery category above, stitching pleat tuck allowance 4½″ from top edge. Form box pleat over stitching; press flat, but *do not* tack folds. Machine-baste top edges of pleats in place (A).

To make tabs, fold strip in half lengthwise; stitch in a ½″ seam (B). Press seam open, being careful not to press creases in tab. Turn tab right side out. Center fabric over seam; press flat (C). Fold tab in half with seam on the inside; baste to panel over each box pleat and at each side where the hem crease will fall (D).

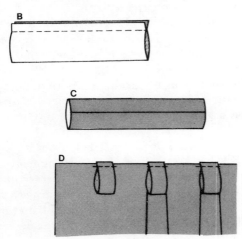

To make facing, place stiffening ½″ below the upper edge; pin and stitch ¼″ from the upper edge of stiffening. Turn in lower facing edge over stiffening and stitch in place through all thicknesses. Stitch facing ends to the side hem edges in a 1½″ seam; press seams toward sides (E). Stitch facing to heading in a ½″ seam (F). Turn facing to the inside, pulling up tabs; press (G).

Finish side and bottom hems as directed in Classic Unlined Draw Draperies procedure #3, steps A and B.

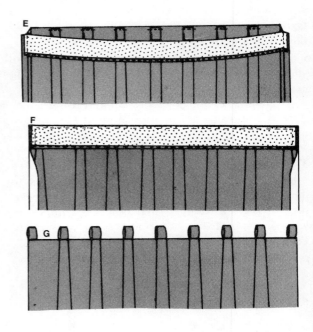

HINT: For some fabrics, it may be necessary to stitch across the spaces between the pleats to hold the facing in place. If needed, stitch ⅛″ from the top edge through all thicknesses.

10. SHIRRED HEADING: This simple decorator touch adds elegance to any fabric and is easier than making pleats. You will need 4-cord shirr-tape the finished width of each drapery plus 4″, and a standard curtain rod.

Calculate yardage and make these draperies as for *Curtains,* procedure #1, or Lined Draw Draperies, procedure #5, allowing 4″ for the *casing* with a heading.

To make a casing with heading, allow for a 1″ heading, doubled; 2″ for casing. *Do not* turn under the free edge of the casing after the heading has been stitched—it will be caught in the stitching when the shirr-tape is stitched in place.

To apply shirr-tape, center over casing with one edge of the tape extending ½″ over the raw edge of the casing; pin (A). With a blunt object, pull out each cord from the tape at the edge of the drapery and turn in each end of the tape to clear the outside of the panel. At one end, tie cords together and knot the opposite cord ends so they do not fray. Stitch above and below each cord through all thicknesses, keeping cords and ends free of stitching (B).

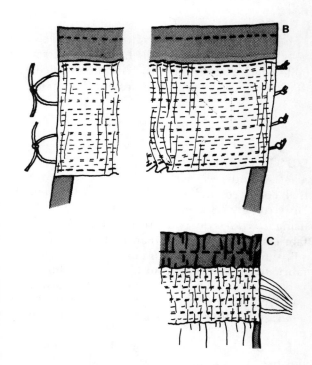

Pull up cords to shirr fabric to fit rod (C). Gather drapery on the rod. Tie long cords together, but *do not* cut off the cords. Distribute the shirring evenly along the cords. Pin extra cord to the back of the drape so it can be released for easy cleaning and pressing after the cords are released.

HINT: Make matching *tiebacks* using the same fullness as for the draperies. Use a 6″-wide fabric strip; turn in the edges ¾″ and press. Stitch shirr-tape to fabric and shirr to the planned length of the tieback.

DRAW DRAPERIES
See *Draperies,* procedures #1 through #6.

DROP

The vertical strips of fabric on a *bedspread, couch cover,* or a *tablecloth* that falls from the mattress or table edge. The drop may be cut in one piece with the top or it may be seamed around the top edges.

DUST RUFFLE

These beauties were invented to hide any dust balls that collected under the bed between cleanings. Dust ruffles are now an important feature when using *coverlet-*style bedspreads or *comforters.* The fabric may be wash-and-wear utilitarian or made of silk, satin, or any decorator fabric. Simply match the fabric to the theme of your bedroom and the wear it will receive. The favorite dust ruffle styles are gathered for a soft look, or smooth with *inverted pleats* at the foot corners for a tailored bed treatment.

Use *Bed Measurements* B and D to calculate the finished measurement to go around the two sides and across the foot end of the springs. Use measurement F to determine how deep to make the dust ruffle.

For a gathered dust ruffle, use 2, 2½, or 3 times the measurement for the three top edges to establish the fullness desired.

For a smooth dust ruffle with inverted pleats, add 31″ to the three top edge measurements for two 12″ sections that will make two 3″ inverted pleats at each foot corner, 2″ for two 1″ hem allowances for the head ends, and 5″ for *ease,* allowing 2″ for each side and 1″ at the foot.

For both styles, add 6″ to measurement F to determine the cut length of the drop—1½″ for a hem allowance and 4½″ so the top edge will extend under the mattress. To accommodate a footboard, see *Bedspreads,* procedure #4, #5, or #6.

1. FOR A GATHERED DUST RUFFLE, you will need about 2 dozen safety pins to secure dust ruffle to box springs and 2-cord shirr-tape the length of the stitched sections, plus 2″. Stitch all widths together; *clean-finish* seam allowances. Turn in ends and bottom edges 1″; press. Turn in raw edge to meet fold; press and stitch hem in place. Turn in top edge 1″; press. Place 2-cord shirr-tape ½″ above the raw edge, extending the ends 1″ beyond the hemmed ends; pin. Using a blunt object, pull out cords at each end and knot. Tuck under raw tape ends; stitch tape to ruffle along top and bottom edges, keeping cords free of stitching.

Pull up cords until dust ruffle fits around the two sides and foot end. Tie cords together securely. Distribute fullness evenly along the cords. Remove mattress. Lap gathered edge over box springs and pin in place at 12″–18″ intervals.

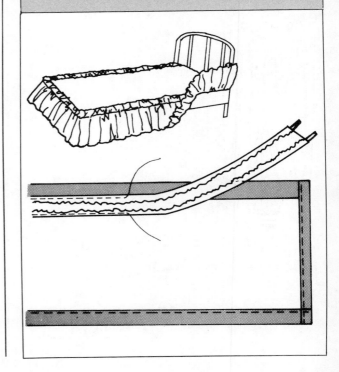

To determine the number of fabric widths needed use:

Measurement B (bed length) _____

For both sides $\times$ ___2___

Plus measurement D (bed width) $+$ _____

Equals perimeter measurement $=$ _____

   For gathered dust ruffle perimeter _____

   Multiply 2, 2½, 3 times for fullness $\times$ _____

   Equals total perimeter measurement $=$ _____

   For smooth dust ruffle perimeter _____

   Plus pleat and ease allowance $+$ ___31___

   Equals total perimeter measurement $=$ _____

Divide your total for dust ruffle perimeter by fabric width: 36″, 44″, 48″, 54″, 60″ $\div$ _____

Equals number of fabric widths $=$ _____

To determine cut length of each fabric width use:

Measurement F (drop length) _____

Add finishing allowance $+$ ___6___

Equals cut length $=$ _____

   For fabric with pattern repeat
   Divide cut length by *pattern repeat* length $\div$ _____

   Equals number of repeats per length. If a fraction remains, round up to the nearest number: $=$ _____

   Multiply by length of repeat $\times$ _____

   Equals adjusted cut length $=$ _____

Your cut length _____

Times the number of fabric widths $\times$ _____

Equals yardage in inches $=$ _____

Divided by 36 $\div$ ___36___

Equals total yardage required for dust ruffle $=$ _____

2. FOR A SMOOTH DUST RUFFLE WITH INVERTED BOX PLEATS, you will need about 2 dozen safety pins to secure dust ruffle to box springs.

Stitch all widths together. Turn in end and bottom edges 1½″; press. Turn in raw edges ½″; stitch hem in place (A). Allowing 2″ on each side and 1″ at the foot for *ease,* form tucks at the foot corners, using 12″ for each. Stitch from top edge for 4½″ (B). Center fabric over stitching forming two 3″-deep pleats. *Machine-baste* top edge in place. Turn down top edge 1″ and hem (C).

Remove mattress. Lap top edge over box springs and pin in place at 12″–18″ intervals. *Miter* corners and pin to support pleats.

DUVET

This European bed treatment, pronounced doo-vay, is fast becoming a favorite with Americans who want to keep bed making to a minimum. The duvet cover is used in place of a top sheet and is like a pillow-case covering for a comforter (usually filled with down that is not washed frequently). If using a duvet to change a color on a comforter, be sure the comforter fabric does not show through the new fabric.

To make a duvet, measure the comforter, adding 5¼″ to the length and 2¼″ to the width. Use sheets or seam both sides to these measurements (see *Pattern Repeats*). With right sides together, stitch the two layers together along the side and top edges in a ⅝″ seam; at bottom corners, stitch in a 3″ seam for 12″–18″, leaving an opening to form the duvet cover (A).

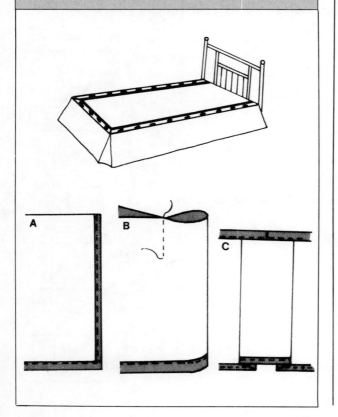

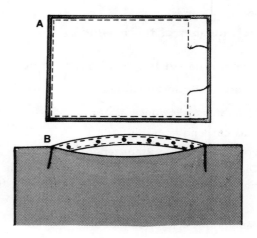

To prepare the opening for a closure of snap tape or *nylon tape fastener,* turn down each wide bottom seam allowance a scant 1″, wrong sides together; press. Turn these pressed edges down again 1″ inch to meet the stitching; press. Separate the pressed edges and turn one pressed edge back over the duvet. Starting and ending ½″ beyond the stitching, place the socket or hook strip of your tape fastener across the opening on the extended pressed edge with one tape edge next to the seam line; pin. Stitch tape in place along both long edges and ends of tape. Align the ball or loop strip on the remaining pressed opening edge; pin. Extend the unstitched edge of the opening and, keeping the duvet free, stitch remaining tape fastener strip in place. Turn duvet right side out; press all edges flat (B). Slide duvet over comforter, matching corners. Secure opening.

HINT: Grosgrain ribbon or self-fabric ties, buttons and buttonholes, sew-on snaps, or hammer-on snaps may also be used to close the opening.

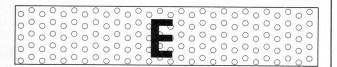

EASE

Style features require additional fullness on one edge of a seam so the fabric will hang free or cup slightly, such as the *drop* on the fitted *bedspreads* or the curved shape of a chair arm. To accommodate this need, one section is made longer along the seam line than the section to which it will be stitched.

To ease, pin sections together at even intervals and divide the excess fabric equally. Place the pins as close as needed to control the excess (sometimes as close as ¼ "). When stitching the seam, stretch the shorter section as you stitch so it will ease smoothly without puckers along the stitching. If the fabric is stiff or heavy, or if there is an excess amount of fabric to be eased, use an *ease-thread* explained below.

EASE-THREAD

Use a slightly longer stitch for an ease-thread (heavy or thick fabric will need a longer stitch length) and stitch from the right side of the fabric, just outside the seam line in the seam allowance, so the ease-thread will not show on the right side of the item. The bobbin thread usually pulls easier and you will be working from the wrong side of the fabric when adjusting the ease-thread.

EDGE FINISHES

To finish the free edges of your decorating projects see *Bias, Corded String Hem, Cording, Fold-over Braid, Fringe, Hems, Ruffles,* and *Trims.*

EDGE-STITCH

After an edge or fold has been pressed flat, you can hold it in place with a row of edge-stitching. Stitch ¹⁄₁₆ "–⅛ " from the edge or fold through all thicknesses.

ELASTICIZED CASINGS

Casings are sometimes elasticized for sink skirts (see *Bathrooms,* procedure #1) and *slipcovers* for flexibility or easy removal. When a *casing* is continuous, leave an opening in its stitching to insert the elastic. After it is inserted, stitch the elastic ends together securely and then stitch the opening shut.

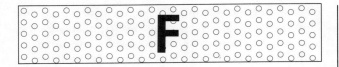

FABRIC HANDLING

The fabric you have selected and purchased will often be the most expensive item needed for the decorating project. Take time to select quality fabric—price does not always guarantee durability. Some luxurious fabrics are meant to be used in formal rooms that do not get a lot of heavy use; others are recommended for an active room.

While in the store, rub fabric between your hands. If fibers come loose or a starchy residue is left on your hands, the fabric will not withstand constant use. When you scratch the surface with a finger nail, the threads should not shift; they should be of uniform diameter without weak or thin areas.

The following fabric characteristics should be resolved before making a purchase to ensure satisfactory results for each and every decorating endeavor:

Has the fabric been treated to be stain resistant or does it have soil-release properties for easy cleaning? This information is usually stamped on the selvage; if it's not, don't be afraid to ask the salesperson.

Is the fabric crease resistant? Permanent-press fabrics are usually crease resistant, too. If you're not sure, try this test: Crush fabric into a tight ball and then release. Do the wrinkles disappear in a short time or do they remain?

Will fabric withstand the wear it will receive? Use delicate, luxurious, or sheer fabrics in rooms that are meant for restricted activities. Use tightly woven, medium- to heavy-weight fabrics for living rooms, bedrooms, and multipurpose rooms that have heavy traffic.

Dry cleaning is usually recommended for decorator fabrics as many are 100 percent cotton. Should you wish to wash the item when it becomes soiled, it is recommended that you shrink the fabric before using (see *Shrinking Fabric*).

Is the fabric colorfast and fade-resistant? Look on the cardboard tube or on the selvage, or ask the salesperson.

Stretch the fabric to see if it will give. You want a firm, unstretchable weave.

Check fabric in natural light. Hold the right side of fabric in the sunlight to see if the color is true under natural light and still compatible with your other colors. Next, hold the fabric up to the sunlight with the right side facing you, to see if the color changes when the light shines through from the wrong side. Any color change is important when matching drapery or any other fabric with your overall color scheme.

Are fabrics finished on the straight grain? Due to the way fabrics are finished with permanent-press, soil-release, polished, and printed surfaces, it is *not* recommended that you try to pull a thread along the straight grain. You must use the fabric as it comes off the bolt. To make a straight line from selvage to selvage, see *Straightening Fabric Ends* and *Pattern Repeats*, procedure #3. Do not purchase fabric or lining that is extremely off-grain as the item will not drape smoothly from top to bottom, and the side hems of curtains or draperies may have a tendency to curl.

Opaque fabrics in light colors may need to be lined to prevent other colors used on beds and furniture from showing through.

Does your project require soft or crisp fabric? Soft fabrics hang straight down in small, soft folds when gathered on a rod or in a seam and are sometimes called limp. Crisp fabrics hang down in puffy, deep, rounded folds when gathered on a rod or in a seam and they are described as stiff or rigid.

Collect fabric in small folds in your hand about a yard from the end and let it hang free. How does it gather, pleat, or drape? If you plan to use lining, lay a length of fabric on a length of lining and make the same test to make sure they are compatible.

If you have answered all these characteristics satisfactorily, but you are still undecided about the color or size of print, buy a yard or two of the fabric. Take the fabric and drape over a bed, chair, or couch or hang it at a window and leave it there for a day or two to see if you still like it. This is a small expenditure compared to the cost of an entire project that may produce unsatisfactory results.

HINT: Some fabric stores have an approval plan whereby you can take the whole fabric bolt home for 24 hours. Many times a small swatch appears to match, but when you see the exact fabric draped in your room, it may not complement the remaining decor.

FABRIC WALLCOVERINGS
See *Wall Hangings* and *Walls*, procedures #1, #2, #3, and #4 for padded upholstered coverings and procedures #1, #2, and #5 for a shirred treatment.

FACE
A term used to direct you to use a *facing* to finish a free edge that is shaped or is not long enough to have a hem folded back for finishing.

FACING
A strip of fabric stitched to an edge for finishing. The inner free edge is *clean-finished* and the opposite edge is stitched in place to the right side of the item. The facing is turned to the inside, pressed flat along the seam, and then stitched in place as for a hem. *Bias binding* and *band trim* are excellent facing substitutes.

FASTENERS
Any item used to allow an opening to be opened and closed at will. Buttons and buttonholes, sew-on hook and eyes, or hook-and-eye tape, nylon tape fastener, *slip-stitching* by hand, sew-on snaps, hammer-on snaps, snap tape, ties, Velcro, and zippers are some of the fasteners that may be used on decorator projects.

FAVOR
A term used to direct you to favor an outside layer of fabric, rolling the inner layer to the inside so it does not show on the outer side when it is positioned.

FESTOON
A term used to describe the decorative folds of fabric that form between two areas and are looped or scalloped to form a graceful trim.

FINIAL
A term used for the decorative ornaments inserted at each end of a drapery or café curtain rod.

FINISHED HEM
A term used to remind you to finish the hem as planned. See *hems* for straight, curved, and corner finishes.

FITTED BEDSPREADS
See *Bedspreads*, procedures #1 through #8.

FLAT BEDSPREADS
See *Bedspreads*, procedures #9 through #12.

FLOUNCE
A term used for a gathered or pleated bedspread drop or the skirt around a chair or couch that is wider than a ruffle.

FOCAL POINT
A term used by decorators for a principal or unique point of interest that catches the eye as soon as you walk into a room.

FOLD-OVER BRAID
A decorative trim used as a substitute for *bias bind-*

ing. It is a quick and easy way to finish tabs and the edges of throws. Simply sandwich the braid over a raw edge with the longest layer underneath and the raw edge just touching the fold crease; pin. Stitch close to inner edge through all thicknesses. To stitch braid around corners and curves, follow the directions given in bias binding.

FRAMING FABRIC FOR PICTURES

See *Picture Framing.*

FRENCH SEAM

See *Seams.* For a quick substitute, see *Clean-finish* step D.

FRINGE

A decorative trim with loose fibers that hangs free. You may use purchased fringe or make your own.

1. TO APPLY PURCHASED TRIM to an edge, see *Trims.*

2. TO MAKE FRINGE on a straight edge of a napkin, place mat, tablecloth, table runner, or pillow, select loosely woven fabric such as linen or kettlecloth. Cut squares or rectangles the desired measurement along the lengthwise and crosswise threads. Pull a thread at the desired depth of fringe (½″–1″). Using matching thread, stitch along the lines formed by the pulled-out thread. Use a small machine stitch to prevent unraveling during laundering. Pull all threads parallel to the reinforcement stitches. A blunt tapestry needle will help to remove stubborn threads.

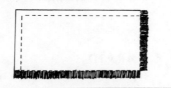

FUSIBLES, FUSIBLE ADHESIVES

To bond two layers together you need a fusible bonding agent that will melt when heat is applied, causing the fabric layers to stick together. Fabric patches may be purchased for mending and appliqué. Fusible interfacing may be used for stiffening; simply iron it on according to package instructions. A fusible webbing is also available to fuse *appliqué, facings,* and *trims* in place instead of stitching.

GARMENT BAGS

Brighten up your closet and protect your clothing with easy-to-make garment bags. For traveling, you may want to add handles and for thick or very full garments, you may want to add a *boxing strip.*

A suit- or jacket-length garment bag requires 2¼ yards of 44″-wide fabric and one 36″ zipper, or two 18″ zippers, for a bag that is about 38″ long. A street-length garment bag requires 2¾ yards of 44″-wide fabric and a 45″ zipper, or two 22″ zippers, for a bag about 45″ long. A floor-length bag requires 3⅜ yards of 44″-wide fabric and a 54″ zipper, or two 27″ zippers, for a bag that is about 59″ long. Be sure to adjust length and yardage to accommodate your particular garment.

For a suit- or jacket-length bag, cut one rectangle 25″ by 40″ for back, two rectangles 13″ by 40″ for front.

For a street-length bag, cut one rectangle 25″ by 47″ for back, and two rectangles 13″ by 47″ for front.

For a floor-length bag, cut one rectangle 25″ by 61″ for back, two rectangles 13″ by 61″ for front.

For all lengths, cut two patches 1¼″ by 5″ for the hanger opening.

Note: All lengths of bag are constructed in the same way. Sketches show the shorter length.

To make zipper opening, turn in the long edges of each front section ½″; press. Place pressed edges alongside the zipper teeth with stop 1″ below the top of the section. (If using two zippers, have pull tabs meet at the center.) Pin the pressed edges to the zipper tape. If zipper(s) is shorter than opening, cut a 2¼″-wide strip twice the length needed. Fold strip in half, wrong sides together; place under pressed edges over the zipper tape ends; pin. Using a zipper foot, stitch pressed edges in place and again about ¼″ away through all thicknesses (A).

To shape the top, fold the back section in half, right sides together. Using a wooden suit hanger, place the center of the hanger along fold. Draw a line on the fabric along the upper edge of the hanger. Slide hanger along the line to fabric edge and continue line, rounding the corner (B). Trim away excess fabric along line (C).

Pin front to back, right sides together, with side and bottom edges even. Trim the front top to match the shape of the back. Unpin these edges. Make hanger opening by turning under the narrow ends ½″; press. At the center of the back and front top edges, stitch one strip to each one in a ¼″ seam (D). Turn patch over raw edge to the wrong side. Turn in the remaining long edge ¼″ and stitch in place through all thicknesses (E).

To assemble, open zipper(s). With right sides together, stitch front to back in a ¼″ seam, starting and ending at the hanger opening (F). Turn right

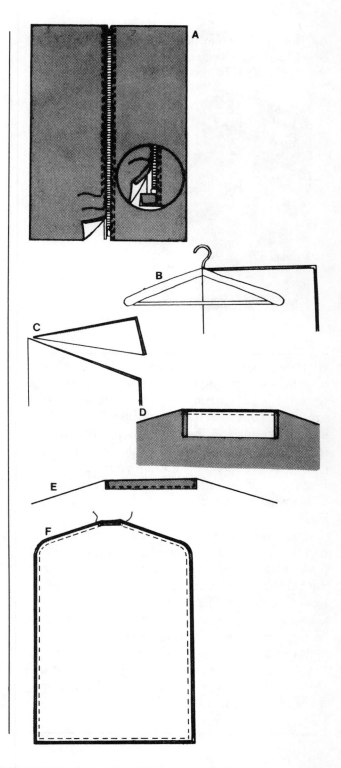

side out; press seam flat. Stitch ¼" from pressed edge, forming a *welting* around the bag edge (G). Put clothing on hanger and store.

HINT: Any size garment bag may be turned into a jumbo storage bag with the addition of an extra wide (15"–18") *boxing strip* made from the same fabric as the rest of the bag. Make the strip long enough to encircle the bag plus 2" for two narrow hems. Be sure to adjust the yardage suggested above to accommodate your boxing strip. Piece the boxing strip as required, using a ¼" seam; zigzag seam allowances together to *clean-finish*.

After steps A, B, and C have been completed and the back has been shaped to match the front, pin boxing strip to front, right sides together, with the hemmed ends lapping ¼" at the center of the front. Stitch boxing strip to front in a ¼" seam. Open zipper(s). Next pin and stitch boxing strip to the back in the same manner.

Turn right side out. Press both seamed edges flat. To form *welting* at each edge of the boxing strip, stitch ¼" from the pressed edges, easing the excess fabric around the corners to fit the bag.

GATHERS

Soft folds along a seam or trim are called gathers and require careful planning to achieve satisfactory results. Select soft, light- to medium-weight fabric as stiff or heavy fabrics will not fall in soft, cascading folds and will fan out, puffing rigidly. The fullness of gathers will depend on their use. The favorite amount of fullness is double the length of the edge to which it is to be joined. Very soft and sheer fabrics look outstanding with triple fullness, but others need only half that amount.

To ensure that threads will not break when pulling up the gathers, use heavy-duty or button and carpet thread on the bobbin, or zigzag over a cord on the wrong side of the fabric. Two rows of gathering threads are needed. Stitch the first row alongside the seam line in the seam allowance and the second row ¼" away, closer to the raw edge.

When gathering long edges, divide the strip into quarters or eighths; mark with pins and break stitches at pins. The heavier the fabric the shorter the gathering threads should be. Make a test scrap to see which type of thread should be used.

For seams with one gathered layer, stitch from the right side of the fabric so the bobbin thread will be on the wrong side.

For applied ruffles with a heading or a double ruffle, stitch from the wrong side of the prepared ruffle strip so the bobbin thread will be on the right side of the fabric. Remove the gathering threads after the ruffle has been stitched in place.

To join a gathering strip to a shorter edge, divide both edges into quarters or eighths; mark with pins. Make gathering threads on longer section as directed above. Pin to shorter section, matching pins. Pull up all gathering threads until they fit the shorter edge. Fasten gathering threads by making a figure eight over the pins. Slide gathers along the threads so they fall evenly between the pins; add more pins and *machine-baste* in place. Stitch seam alongside inner gathering thread and again ¼"

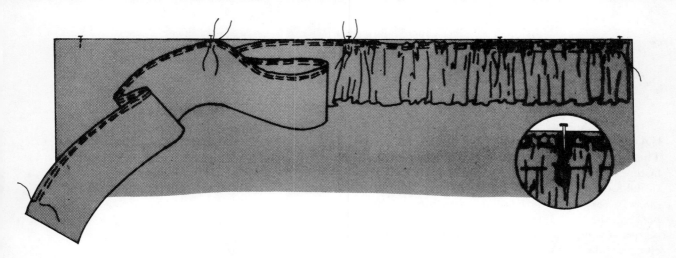

away in the seam allowance to help support the weight of the gathered section. Press gathered folds flat in the seam allowance only.

GLASS CURTAINS

Any style of straight, full-length sheer curtains that hang next to the window glass are called glass curtains. To make sheer glass curtains see *Curtains,* procedure #1, or *Draperies,* procedure #3 for Classic Unlined Draw Draperies with instructions for sheer fabric. The curtain section also has instructions for café, casement, and hourglass curtains.

GRADED SEAMS

To reduce bulk and make a flat finished edge, seam allowances (especially those involving facing) sometimes needs to be graded. Trim away excess seam allowances in layers of graduated width. Start with ⅛"–¼" of one seam allowance, then *clip* and *notch* curves and *trim* corners.

GRAIN

Woven fabrics have two sets of threads interwoven at right angles. The lengthwise threads (grain) run up and down in the same direction as the selvage and the crosswise threads (grain) run back and forth between the selvages. You may be directed to place fabric with the grain running either lengthwise or crosswise.

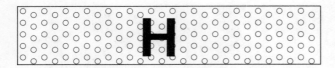

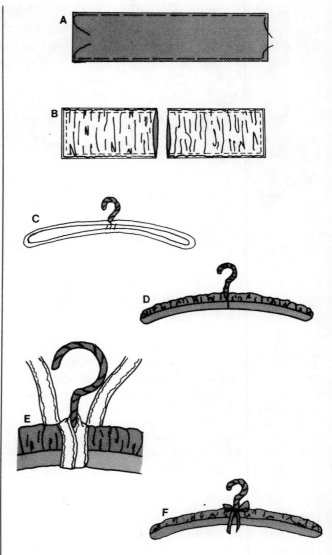

HAND SEWING

There are times when you really need to hem or fasten something by hand for an elegant professional look. At other times, hand sewing is the easiest way to gather or ease an extra-heavy fabric. *Back-stitching* is a durable method used for seams before sewing machines were invented, and some elegant fabrics look best with the zipper back-stitched in place. *Slip-stitching* is often quicker and less expensive then other closures. Blind-hemming is explained in *Hemming Stitches* and hand-basting is explained in *Basting.*

HANGERS

Cover your narrow wooden hangers with padding and cotton, corduroy, or velvet to prevent a garment from stretching or slipping off the hanger. Use fabric scraps, ½"-thick foam or batting for padding, 1"-wide ribbon 27" long for a bow or 16" for a knot, and color-coordinated plastic tape to wrap hook.

Cut two fabric strips about 2½" by 9" and two about 2½" by 14" for the cover. Cut one strip of foam about 2" by 32" or batting about 4" by 33" for padding.

Make covers by adding a row of gathering threads ¼" from both long edges of the longest strip (A). Pin these strips to the remaining ones. Adjust gathers and distribute evenly. Add more pins as needed. Stitch long edges and one end in a ¼" seam (B).

Wrap hook from tip to base with plastic tape, pulling tight as you work. Pad hanger with a strip of batting folded in half lengthwise or with foam. Wrap padding strip around narrow edge of hanger, with edges meeting at the hook. Fold padding over flat sides and staple the padding in place (C).

Turn covers right side out and slip one over each end of the hanger, crushing padding tight as you work. Lap raw ends where they meet around the hook (D). Loop ribbon over hook and wrap down over the raw edges. Bring ribbon up around on the back (E) and tie into a bow or knot at the front of the hook (F).

HEADBOARDS

There are many ways to make a headboard or backrest for a distinctive decorator look. Make free-hanging headboards, upholster a wall behind the bed (see *Walls*, procedures #1, #2, #3, and #4), add a short canopy, or slipcover your present headboard. Make a matching or contrasting headboard treatment or use a combination of several ideas.

1. FREE-HANGING HEADBOARD.

Use wooden or metal poles to hang this style of headboard or backrest after fabric tabs have been inserted into one edge of a box-edge cushion with a foam form, using fabric that matches the bedspread or couch. *Anchor* pole so the cushion(s) hang free of the bed pillows or couch edge. Cushioned headboards or backrests may be 2"–3" thick. Keep the proportions in scale with the furniture.

Tab hangers are made the same as for Stationary Draperies with Tab Hangers found in *Draperies*, procedure #8. Make *Box-edge Cushions*, using procedure #1, basting tabs to boxing strip, or procedure #2 or #3, inserting tabs in the seam.

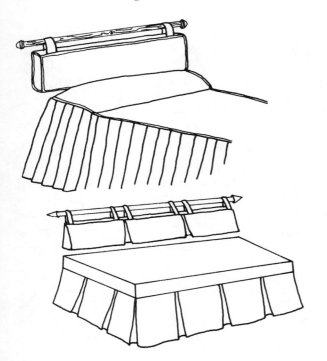

2. SLIPCOVERED HEADBOARD.

Change the look of your headboard with a slipcover. You may want to use an old mattress cover, a blanket, or batting to soften the edges by wrapping the padding around the headboard and stapling or hand sewing it in place. Or you may make a padded layer the same as for a slipcover as explained below.

To make slipcover, pad headboard if desired. Use two strips of fabric the length of the headboard, plus ends and seam allowances. To the depth of the headboard allow enough fabric to tuck behind the mattress plus seam and hem allowances. Pin top and side edges, right sides together, following the lines of the headboard. Stitch the two layers together following the pins (trim seam allowance to ⅝"). Or draw a line along the pins and add a seam allowance if you want to add *cording* and/or a *boxing strip* to the side and top edges. Narrow hem bottom edges.

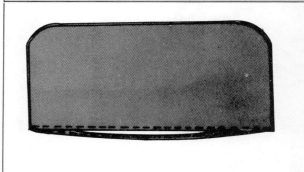

HEADING

The term heading is used for two types of decorating finishes. It may describe a ruffled edge created above a casing when a rod, elastic, or a drawstring is used to gather the casing. The finished top of curtains and draperies and the narrow free edge of a ruffle are also referred to as headings.

HEMMING STITCHES

Use one of the following methods to make your hem stitches nearly invisible. To prepare hem, turn in the raw hem edge ½"; pin. Then, pin hem in place.

For a machine-sewn blind-hemming stitch, follow instructions given for your machine using the following tips. When pinning hem in place, insert pins about ⅛" from inner hem fold. Turn back hem along the pins so the hem edge extends about ⅛" beyond the fold. Using the blind-hem stitch, stitch alongside the fold, catching just a thread or two with the extended stitch. Pull hem down and press (A).

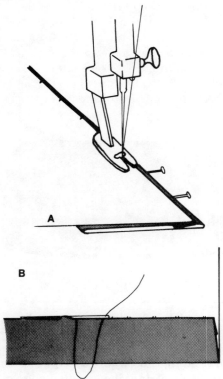

For a hand-sewn blind-hemming stitch, work from right to left. Knot thread and hide under fold. Slip needle through folded edge; swing needle to pick up a fiber thread of the fabric alongside the hem edge. Pull up thread and repeat this step, making the stitches in the fold about ¼" apart (B).

HEMS

These folded edge finishes do not always have a straight edge and need some help to make a smooth, flat inner edge. Turn in the raw edge ½"; press. Stitch hem in place through all thicknesses or *clean-finish* raw hem allowance edge as desired and use one of the *hemming stitches* above to secure the hem.

1. STRAIGHT HEM. Turn up hem allowance; press. Turn in raw hem ½"; stitch hem in place (A).

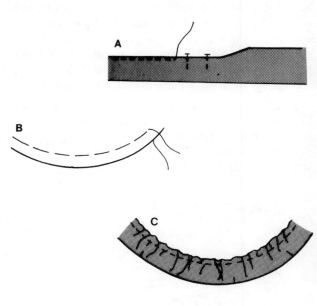

2. CURVED HEM. To make inner hem edge fit, use the longest machine stitch and stitch ¼"–½" from the curved edge (B). Turn up hem allowance; pin. Turn in the raw edge along the stitching; pull up thread to ease in fullness. Stitch hem in place; press (C).

3. CORNER HEM: For light- to medium-weight fabrics, turn in the corners at a 45-degree angle where they meet (A). Fold in long edges where they meet at an angle at the corner (B). Trim away excess fabric at corner; stitch hem in place.

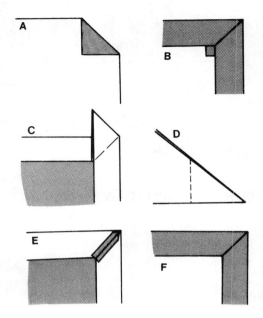

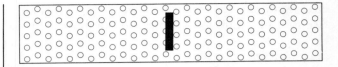

For heavy or bulky fabrics, turn hem allowances to the outside at the corner. Pinch the edges together where they meet. Make diagonal creases at the corners (C). Bring creases together and stitch together along the crease (D). Trim away excess to within ¼″ of the stitching; press seam open with tip of iron, being careful not to press hem fold (E). Turn hem allowance to inside; press (F). Complete hem as desired.

For other hem finishes, see *Corded String Hem, Cording, Fringe, Trims,* and *Ruffles.*

HIGH-RISER (PULL-OUT) COUCH COVER
See *Couch Covers.*

HOBBLED SHADE
See *Roman Shades,* procedure #8.

HOURGLASS CURTAINS
See *Curtains,* procedure #4.

INSULATION

As you consider each decorating project, it may be possible to insulate around your doors and windows to prevent heat loss in cold weather and an overworked air conditioner during the hot weather. Draperies that stand away from walls and that are not closed in at the top encourage energy loss. We all know warm air rises and draperies hung this way form a tunnel between the glass and the drape that draws the warm air down toward the cold glass, cooling the air. This cold air filters down to the floor, causing the heating equipment to go into operation. As the air is warmed it rises and the same cycle starts all over again. In warm weather, an air conditioner reverses this cycle. An opened window behind drapes forces the warm air upward, causing the same cycle by bringing in warm outside air.

Draperies are the easiest to adapt to prevent energy loss when lined with an insulated lining, then hung from the ceiling with traditional rods that allow the drapes just to touch the ceiling and extend from one side of the wall to the other. You may also anchor the drapery's side edges to the wall with pushpins, staples, nylon fastener tape, or magnetic strips. When ceiling draperies are not used, the top of the draperies must be covered with a *cornice* or *lambrequin.*

Flat *Roman shades* are quite popular as energy savers when they are lined with an insulated lining. They may be used alone or with draperies. Those that are mounted close to the glass, flat against the window frame, or held close with magnetic strips or tracks are the most efficient. For a daytime bare window look, shades fold neatly at the top looking very much like a *valance.* Or place the shade behind *stationary draperies,* a *cornice,* or *lambrequin.* Even the traditional window shade will help prevent some energy loss when mounted next to the glass.

Screens and panels are another way to create a

barrier to prevent energy loss when placed in your window or sliding glass door indentation.

Insulated Lining: There are many types of insulated linings on the market that will give you excellent results. Be aware that no matter how carefully you insulate your window treatment, if it is not mounted as explained in *insulation* above, you will not save as much on energy.

Some linings have a layer of insulated material bonded to the fabric that will drape well and be compatible with decorator fabrics. A currently popular multilayered insulated fabric has several layers of barrier materials stitched to the lining fabric. It works extremely well for flat *Roman shades* and *screens* and as a flat draw drapery (finished as in *Draperies*, procedure #5, eliminating the pinch pleats, and hung on the traverse rod with pin hooks, making rolling folds at the heading).

INTERFACING

An additional layer of stiffening fabric used to help hold shapes on fabric that may otherwise droop. Use *fusible* (iron-on) or sew-in interfacing on soft fabrics along scalloped or shaped edges that should be crisp.

INTERLINING

A layer of flannel type fabric used in draperies as an insulation. To interline, cut same as lining. Baste the two layers together and handle as one throughout construction.

INVERTED PLEATS

Used singly, inverted pleats are found at corners of *bedspreads*, *couch covers*, or *dust ruffles*. Many times they are used in combination with *box pleats* for a pleated drop. See *Pleats.*

INWARD

A term used to describe a concave curve or corner that forms an edge. See *Bias, Clip, Hems,* and *Trims.*

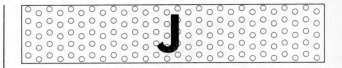

JABOT

A cascade of shaped fabric or ruffles that hangs in a cone or graduated pleated shape. Usually used with a draped *valance.*

JOINING FABRIC WIDTHS

See *Pattern Repeats,* procedure #4.

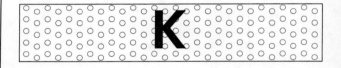

KNIFE PLEATS

A continuous row of narrow pleats with the folds all going in the same direction. The term "knife pleats" is used because the creases are pressed into sharp edges. See *Bedspreads* and *Pleats.*

KNIFE-EDGE PILLOWS

These flat pillows are the easiest to make because they are thick in the center and taper to nothing at the outer edge, requiring only one seam around the perimeter. This one-seam pillow is called a knife-edge pillow, while the *box-edge cushion* or pillow requires provisions for its thickness and usually needs two seams. Use two pieces of fabric, one for the top and another for the bottom. A beautiful decorator fabric may need only a plain edge; others will take a decorative seam in stride. Add a Sunburst Top (procedure #6 below) or use *cording, ruffles,* or *trim* in the seam for added interest.

Needlework artists will find the knife-edge pillow a perfect way to add *accent colors* while showing off their handiwork. When constructing a pillow with a needlework top, back it with a durable layer of fabric to prevent stress. Simply cut a piece of *backing* fabric the same size as needed for the pillow and baste it to the wrong side of the needlework. Handle the two layers as one during construction.

Use a purchased pillow form or make one to your measurements, using white or natural-colored inexpensive fabric, or an old sheet, and fill it with polyester fiberfill stuffing or foam chips.

For a perfect circle, make a pattern using a pushpin, pencil, and string. Cut a groove in the pencil near the point and tie a string around the groove. Place a thick magazine under paper for pattern. Weight the corner or tape in place. Tie string to pin, making the distance between pencil point and pin one-half the diameter. Insert pin into magazine at the center of paper; draw circle. Example: For a finished 14″ cover, the diameter is 15″ (including two ½″ seam allowances) so the distance between the pin and point should be 7½″.

To measure a purchased form, measure the length and width (A) for rectangles and squares. Measure the diameter for circles (B). Add 1″ to each measurement for two ½″ seam allowances.

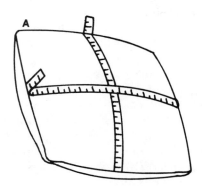

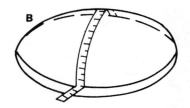

1. TO MAKE A CLASSIC KNIFE-EDGE PILLOW COVER, cut two fabric pieces the desired shape. Squares and rectangles can be drawn on the wrong side of the fabric with pencil and ruler. Be sure the edges are squared with the design. Make a circle pattern as described above. To use a zipper closure, see procedure #2 below before cutting out the fabric. Baste any decorative edging to the right side of the top and use a *slip-stitch* closure.

Pin the two rectangular (A), square, or circular (B) pieces together; stitch in a ½″ seam leaving an opening for form. Turn right side out, shaping edges. Insert form, matching corners and edges (C). *Slip-stitch* opening shut, following step B or C.

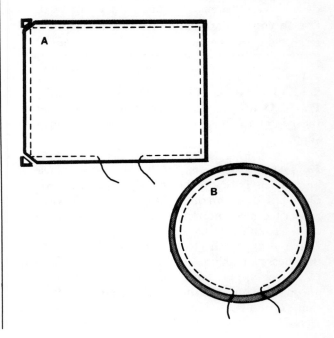

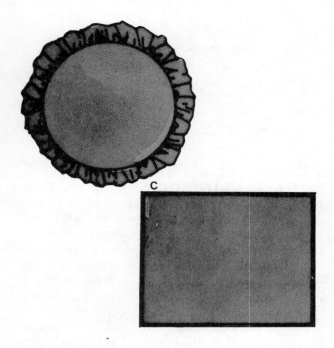

over zipper, keeping ends of top and bottom even; stitch ¼″ from pressed edge (B). *Open zipper now!* You don't want to stitch the remaining edges together and not be able to turn the cover right side out. Fold top over bottom, right sides together and raw edges even. Make sure zipper tape ends are even at opening ends. Stitch remaining edges together as directed in procedure #1 above.

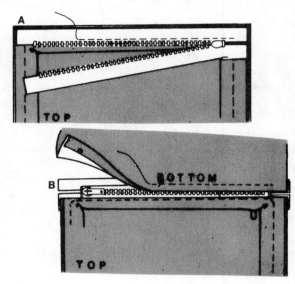

HINT: To eliminate exaggerated or floppy corners, make stitching at each corner about ¼″ deeper (¾″ seam allowance) tapering back to the original ½″ seam allowance 2″–4″ beyond each side, depending on the pillow size.

2. ZIPPER CLOSURES FOR PILLOWS

may be inserted at one edge or in the center of the bottom for circles and unusual shapes.

For squares and rectangles, baste trim in place (if being used) to one section for the top. Open zipper, place face down on the right side of the top with the zipper teeth extending over the basting for the trim or ½″ from raw edge on a plain top; pin. Using a zipper foot, stitch close to the teeth through all thicknesses, making sure zipper tab can slide easily (A). Close zipper. Turn zipper tape and seam allowance under top. On the matching edge of the bottom, turn in this edge ½″; press. Pin pressed edge

For round or unusual shapes, insert zipper in the center of the bottom section. First, cut out the top. Then fold pattern in half and add ⅝″ to this straight edge for the opening seam allowances. Cut two sections for bottom as needed. Turn in one bottom section ½″ along the straight opening edge; press. Place folded edge over zipper tape along the teeth, leaving enough room for the zipper tab to pull easily; pin. Using a zipper foot, stitch close to pressed edge (A). Next, turn in the remaining straight edge ¾″; press. Center over zipper with pressed edge along the stitching on the first section, aligning the outer edge so the bottom matches the top in shape; pin to zipper tape. Stitch zipper in place (B). *Open zipper now!* Stitch outer edges together as directed in procedure #1 above.

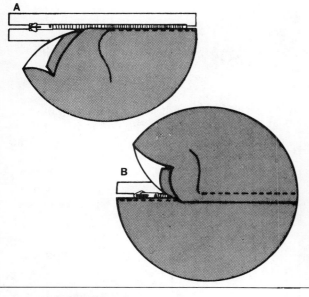

3. QUICK AND EASY MACHINE-SEWN PILLOW COVERS: Finish knife-edge pillows with a *welting* or a 2″ flange edge, stitching openings shut by machine for fast completion.

For a welted edge, add 1½″ to measurement A and B or C for two ½″ seam allowances and two ¼″ welting allowances. Stitch top and bottom together as directed in procedure #1 above. After turning the cover right sides out, press seamed edges flat. Stitch a scant ¼″ from pressed edge, forming welting (A). Insert form. Turn in openings ½″; press. Pin folded edges together. Stitch opening shut, connecting with previous welting stitches (B).

For a 2″ flange edge, add 5″ to measurements A and B or C for two 2″ flanges and two ½″ seam allowances. Stitch top and bottom together as directed in procedure #1 above. After turning the cover right side·out, press seamed edges flat. Stitch close to pressed edges and 2″ inside the pressed edges between opening (C). Insert form. Turn in opening edges ½″; press. Pin folded edges together. Complete flange stitching, keeping form free, and stitch opening shut, connecting with previous stitching (D).

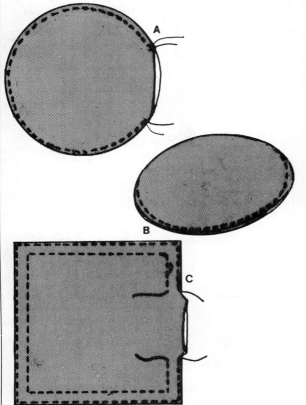

4. HAREM CORNERS: Measure form and then cut top and bottom as in procedure #1 above. *Slip-stitch* closure—step B is recommended. When using a zipper, make it 4″ shorter than the edge. Stitch top to bottom as in procedure #1. Before turning right side out, tie each corner. Using 2 strands of doubled thread in needle, tie a knot about 3″ from end of thread. Insert needle about 1½″ from corner alongside the stitching in the seam allowance. Keeping tail free, wrap thread tightly around the fabric several times and tie securely. Repeat for all four corners. Turn right side out, fanning gathers so they will accommodate the form. Insert form, matching corners, and close opening.

5. NO-SEW PILLOW OR CUSHION COVERS: For a quick change, use a scarf or a piece of fabric about three times the length and width of the pillow. For a tied cover, center form on fabric as shown (A). Fold sides over form, tucking excess underneath (B). Bring remaining corners together and tie into a square knot over the center (C). For a pinned cover, center form lengthwise and crosswise (D); tuck in the raw ends and pin the top layers together securely on the underneath side with safety pins (E).

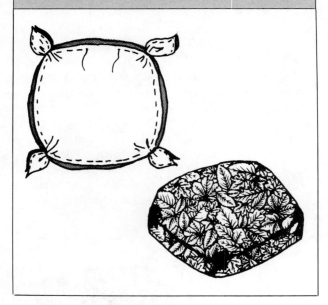

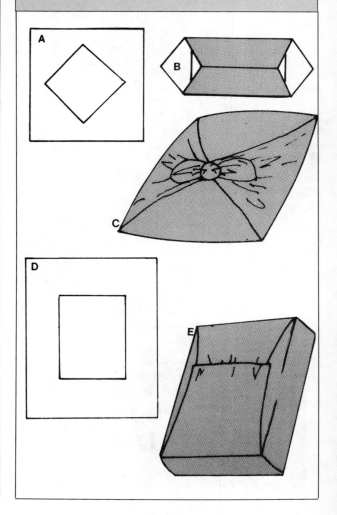

6. SUNBURST PILLOW COVER: To make an unusual round pillow cover, use a strip of fabric 1½ to 2 times the length of the circumference of your pillow, plus 1″ for two seam allowances, matching fabric for pillow back and muslin or an old white sheet for backing. Use a trim around the outer edge and two large buttons or button forms covered with self-fabric. Cut out strip, pillow back, and backing for top as explained in the beginning of this Knife-edge Pillow section. Stitch narrow ends of strips in a ½″ seam. Divide strip into quarters; mark both edges with pins. Gather both edges between the pins.

Divide backing into quarters, mark with pins. Place wrong side of strip over backing, matching pins, and repin at these points. Pull up gathers to fit backing; secure ends. Distribute gathers evenly; baste (A). At the center, pull up gathers as tight as possible. If your fabric is bulky, baste in place by hand, easing in the excess, then stitch securely to the backing by machine. Baste cording to top over gathers (B) and stitch top to bottom as in procedure #1 above. Insert form and *slip-stitch* opening shut. Thread a long needle with double button or carpet thread, and tie to one button shank, leaving a 3″ tail. Insert needle through pillow, then through remaining button shank. Reinsert needle about ¼″ from first threads to the front of the pillow. Repeat procedure (C). Pull thread taut, forming dimples on both sides of pillow. Knot securely and cut tie ends to ½″ (D).

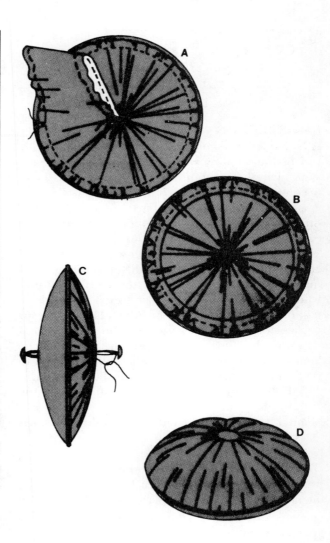

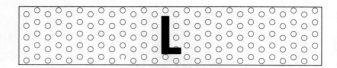

LAMBREQUIN

A boxed frame, similar to a *cornice*, that covers the top of the window with sides that extend to the same length as your window treatment. Lambrequins are considered energy savers. Be sure *draperies* and *Roman shades* have enough clearance on the inside of the lambrequin to stack and move easily.

Measure width of window at top of any trim and at the sill, adding to the width for stacking if required. Measure length from top of trim or spot where lambrequin should start to the place where it should end (sill, apron, or floor). Hang rods for curtains or draperies or measure the thickness and depth of the folds as they would hang behind the lambrequin. You will need these measurements to determine the inside measurements of the box. Use ½″–1″-thick lumber, making the sides and top 6″–10″ deep and the front 10″–12″ wide. For a shaped front, enlist the aid of a friend with a compass saw.

To make lambrequin frame, use wood glue and nails to fasten box together and 4 mending plates (2 at each place where the front top and sides are joined). Glue and nail the side and top boxing frame together (A). Join front sections together with mending plates (B). With mending plates on the inside, glue and nail front to the frame (C).

Match fabric designs as explained for *Pattern Repeats* when seaming widths for a wider lambrequin. Striped fabrics look great when chevroned at the top front corners. Pad and cover lambrequin as for a *Cornice*, procedure #1, then hang with *angle iron* brackets, using at least three on each side and top; *anchor* screws to walls or studs. If the inside of the lambrequin is visible from the outside, such as for a sliding glass door, be sure to cover with matching

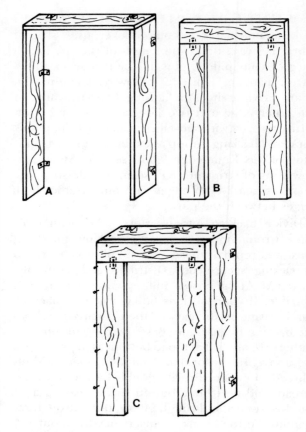

fabric for a complete decorator look. You may want to cover that last row of staples with a strip of decorative trim glued over them.

LAMPSHADES

When lampshades become soiled or faded, or if they are the wrong color, it is often hard to find a replacement shade because of the proportions. Fabric and paint are often the easiest ways to restore them. Try to use the same color intensity for the lampshade when redoing it so you will have the same effect and efficiency as the original shade. Reclaiming bent and/or ripped shades is not worth your time as a damaged covering may show through new coverings, and bent frames will never hold the shade on the lamp satisfactorily. You can recover your shade with a permanent or removable method.

1. PERMANENT METHOD.

Almost any stable fabric can be used to cover a lampshade. Decorator fabrics, textured silks, and other fabrics can be glued to a shade. It is even possible to paint shades and then cover them with open-weave or eyelet embroidery fabric. Wipe the shade clean to remove dust and dirt. Do a patch test to make sure the fabric can be glued successfully. When painting a shade, use a thin coat and don't use a dark color that will affect the light efficiency.

To make a pattern, lay lampshade on paper. Starting at the seam, draw a line the length of the shade. Then mark the top and bottom edges. Roll shade over paper, marking both top and bottom edges as it is moved, ending again at the seam. Smooth out lines (A). Cut out pattern with a 1″ margin. Place pattern on lampshade and check fit, lapping the ends ½″. The lines should be even with both edges of the shade. Add ½″ to the side and bottom edges for a wrap-around and to one end for lapping. When pattern is complete, pin to fabric as shown (B).

To attach fabric, remove any decorative trim from the shade. *Do not* remove the thin paper that holds the shade to the frame. Apply glueing agent to shade, following manufacturer's directions for white craft glue or a spray adhesive. Make sure all areas are covered or those spots will look dull. Fabric will dry clear. Before glue dries, apply fabric, starting at the seam and centering it. Smooth fabric around the shade, overlapping and glueing these ends (C). Glue top and bottom shade edges continuing to the inside about ¼″; smooth fabric over the edges to the inside of the shade, making short *clips* at even intervals so the fabric will be smooth (D). To add trim, start at seam. Try to match the ends by easing or stretching the trim to fit.

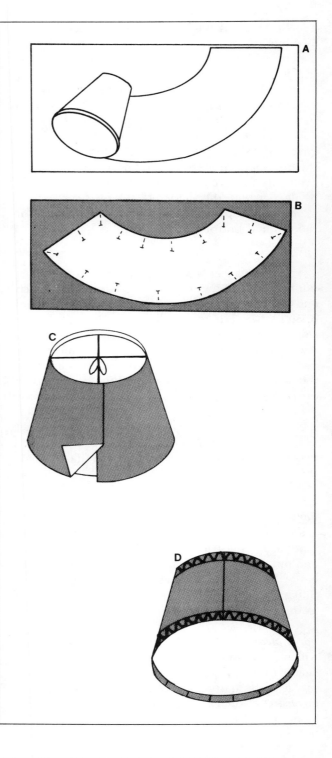

2. REMOVABLE METHOD. Test fabric by draping it over the shade with the light on to see the effect after the cover is attached. Some pleated and gathered covers may cut down on the light if made with dark colors or heavy fabric.

Lampshade covers are attached to the shade with nylon tape fastener or snap tape. For a gathered cover, cut a fabric rectangle twice the circumference of the shade bottom; for a pleated cover, triple the bottom circumference, adding 1″ to both measurements for two ½″ seam allowances. Cut strip 3″ deeper than the shade (1″ so cover can extend ½″ beyond top and bottom edges and 1″ each for the top and bottom finishes).

To prepare fabric for cover, cut out rectangle to the required measurements. Stitch ends in a ½″ seam, forming a tube; press seam open (A). Turn in top and bottom edges 1″, wrong sides together; press. On the bottom edge, make a narrow hem by tucking the raw edge in to meet fold; press and stitch in place (B). The remaining half of the tape will be applied after the top is gathered or pleated.

Glue tape to top of lampshade, using the hook strip of the nylon tape fastener or the ball section of the snap tape (C).

For a gathered cover, add two or more rows of gathering threads ½″ below the top the width of the tape fastener. Divide tape and cover into quarters and pin cover to tape, matching pins. Pull up gathers to fit; distribute gathers evenly along the tape. Stitch cover to tape close to both tape edges. Trim as desired (D).

For a pleated cover, form knife pleats so the cover will be smooth around the bottom of the lampshade; press. Place tape fastener ½″ below the top; pin at each quarter. Pin each pleat to tape, easing cover to fit; stitch in place close to both edges. Trim as desired (E).

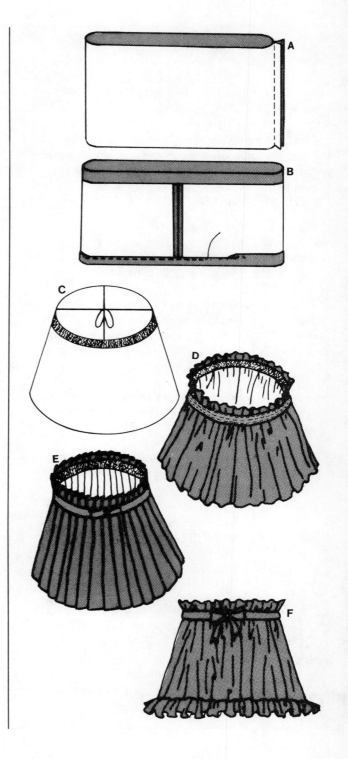

For both styles, add trim to cover stitching with self-fabric or ribbon, making a bow for an added touch. Add *fringe* or self-fabric *ruffles* to gathered style (F).

LAP
A term used to direct you to place one layer of fabric or trim over the bottom layer so the layers overlap for a short distance.

LINED BEDSPREAD
See *Bedspreads* for Fitted Style, procedure #8 and Flat Style, procedure #12.

LINED DRAPERIES
See *Draperies,* for Lined Draw Draperies, procedure #5, and Lined-to-edge Draperies, procedure #8.

MACHINE-BASTING
See *Basting,* procedure #1.

MACHINE BLIND-STITCH
See *Hemming Stitches* step B.

MACHINE QUILTING
See *Quilting By Machine.*

MATCHING STRIPES, PLAIDS, AND PRINTS
See *Pattern Repeats.*

MEASURING BEDS
To measure beds for bedspreads and dust ruffles, see *Bed Measurements.*

MEASURING WINDOWS
When measuring for *Austrian shades, cornices, curtains, draperies, lambrequins,* or *Roman shades,* measure accurately as the yardage is figured by the actual finished width and length desired. Sliding glass doors are measured like a window.

Curtains, draperies, and *shades* may be hung in the window indentation or on the outside next to the trim or wall. For an outside treatment, extend each side at least 4″ beyond the window (8″ total) and at least 4″ above so the rod or board can be hung above the glass. Decorators say there are only three lengths that complement structural lines: floor length, apron length, and sill length.

Determine where you want the window treatment to fall on the wall and whether to hang it above the window or sliding glass door on the wall, or on the ceiling. Use curtains and/or draperies with or without a *cornice, lambrequin,* or *valance* to widen a narrow window, frame a picture window, or cover an undesirable view.

1. INDENTED INSTALLATION. For the width measurement, measure across the window between the side edges of the indentation (A). For the length measurement, measure from the top of the indentation to the sill (B).

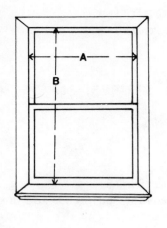

2. OUTSIDE INSTALLATION WITH RODS.

For the width measurement, measure from wall to wall along each return (C) and the front span (D). For draw draperies, see *Curtain and/or Drapery Rods,* procedure #2. For the length measurement, measure from the top of the rod to the sill (E), apron (F), or floor (G).

3. OUTSIDE INSTALLATION FOR SHADES OR WITHOUT RODS.

For the width measurement, measure across the window between the inner edges of trim (H), adding at least 8″ for extensions. For the length measurement, measure from the inner edge of the window trim at the top to the sill (I), apron (J), or floor (K), adding at least 4″ to the measurement.

For sash curtains, measure from the top of the lower sash to the sill (L).

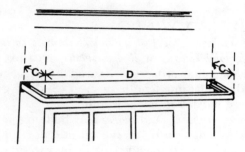

MENDING PLATES

These flat metal rectangles with holes for screws come in many lengths and widths. They are used to reinforce broken boards, or to join similar thicknesses of wood such as for a *lambrequin.* Corrugated nails and Scotch wood joiners may be used where less strain is put on the wood such as joinings for *Screens.*

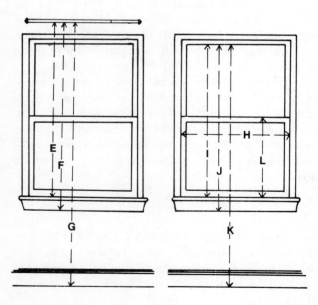

METRIC MEASUREMENTS

It is a good idea to familiarize yourself with the metric system as most of the world uses this form of measurement. Why not purchase a tape measure with inches on one side and centimeters on the other? The metric system is based on units of ten, just like the dollar: 10 millimeters (mm) equal 1 centimeter (cm); 100 centimeters equal 1 meter (m). Use the chart below to become familiar with measurements used for all sorts of crafts. They are transposed to the nearest millimeter.

Inches	Millimeters (mm)	Centimeters (cm)
⅛ ″	3mm	0.3cm
¼ ″	6mm	0.6cm
⅜ ″	10mm	1.0cm
½ ″	13mm	1.3cm
⅝ ″	16mm	1.6cm
¾ ″	19mm	1.9cm
1″	25mm	2.5cm
2″	51mm	5.1cm
3″	76mm	7.6cm
4″		10.2cm
5″		12.7cm
6″		15.2cm
7″		17.8cm
8″		20.3cm
9″		22.9cm
10″		25.4cm
11″		27.9cm
12″		30.5cm

YARDS	CENTIMETERS(cm)	METERS(m)
⅛	11.3cm	
¼	22.6cm	
⅜	34.1cm	
½	45.7cm	
⅝	57.0cm	
¾	68.5cm	
⅞	79.9cm	
1	91.3cm	
1⅛		1.03m
2		1.85m
3		2.75m
4		3.70m
5		4.60m

MITER

A miter is used to make a square corner in fabric or decorative trim. It is formed by a fold or seam at a 45-degree angle. To use mitering, see *Bias Binding, Hems,* procedure #2, and *Trims.*

MOLLY BOLT

A screw and anchor for hollow walls. See *Anchor.*

MOTIF

A dominant and recurring form, shape, or figure printed or woven in a fabric. To match more than one fabric width, see *Pattern Repeats.*

NAP

A term primarily used for fabric that has short fuzzy fibers on the surface such as corduroy and velvet. These fibers slant slightly, reflecting light in a dull or bright manner depending on which way the fabric is viewed. Many smooth, *solid-colored fabrics* such as satin and polished cotton, reflect light in the same way as a napped fabric. To see if your fabric will reflect light, hold it over your body with the cut end under your chin and look down over it in a well-lighted room. Reverse the fabric so it falls in the opposite direction. If one way is bright and the other way is dull, the fabric has a napped finish. One-way prints should be handled the same way.

When cutting napped fabrics, be sure to mark the top edge of all panels for draperies, bedspreads, etc., to save time and grief. Use a soft lead pencil to write the word "top" on the wrong side or mark sheer and delicate fabrics with safety pins.

NAPKINS, PLACE MATS, AND TABLE RUNNERS

Add the ultimate touch to a beautifully set table with custom-made napkins, place mats, or table runners. Napkins do not have to be finished like the other table linens as long as they complement the table and its setting. There are many ways to make napkins, place mats, and table runners, and all may be finished in the same manner. Trim the edges with commercial bias tape or *bias binding*. *Trim* or add an *appliqué* in one corner (A). Use self- or contrasting *Ruffles* for an elegant finish (B).

Many ready-made napkins have a corded edge. To make a similar finish, use the *corded string hem*. Reinforce each side of the corner with a bar-tack by making three stitches in the same holes by dropping

feeddog on the sewing machine. Stitch over cord to corner, make bar-tack ending with needle inserted on the napkin side of the cord. Raise presser foot and pivot napkin on needle so the opposite side of corner is ready to be stitched. Make bar-tack and continue to the next corner (C). To make a self-fringe, see *Fringe*, procedure #2.

NEEDLEBOARD

This pressing tool is constructed with ¼ " long needle-like wires protruding upright through a thick canvas bed. Use a needleboard to press velvet, corduroy, or other pile fabrics to avoid crushing the loose fibers that form the right side of these fabrics.

NEEDLES

Hand-sewing or machine needles must be fine enough to slip through lightweight fabrics and large enough to accommodate thicker threads for some heavy fabrics. Ball-point and special-knit needles are available for your machine so you do not break the fibers on delicate wovens and certain knits. Leather and some leatherlike fabrics require special hand-sewing and machine needles to aid in stitching.

NEUTRALIZING COLORS

Black and gray are made when all the *primary colors* are mixed. These colors are used to make the colors dull or bright. White appears to be a color without hue to most laymen, but a small percentage of gray is used so the color will reflect light.

NONWOVEN

These unusual fabrics are made by pressure, heat, and chemicals. They do not fray or ravel and have no grain so they can be cut in any direction. Felt and interfacing are the most widely used nonwoven fabrics. An elegant suede-look fabric first made popular by an American dress designer is now being used by furniture manufacturers—and it's washable!

NOTCH

A term used to direct you to take out small notches of fabric to eliminate bulk and ridges in a seam allowance when an outside curve is faced. To find out how much must be notched away, turn the seam allowance to the finished position. The ripples that form indicate the excess fabric that needs to be removed. Pinch ripples together and trim away V-shaped wedges, being careful not to cut the stitching.

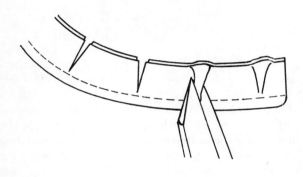

NOTIONS

Buttons, cord, fasteners, measuring and marking tools, needles, pins, thread, and many more items are available in stores that sell supplies for seamstresses and tailors. Notions can add to the cost of your decorating project, so purchase only those you need.

NYLON TAPE FASTENERS

This type of closure has two strips that fasten to each other with one strip used on each side of the opening. One strip has a looplike pile surface and the other has a tiny hooklike surface that clings to the other strip when pressed together. The most common brand name is Velcro.

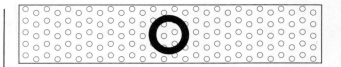

OPAQUE FABRICS

A term used throughout this book for fabric that does not allow light to pass through.

OPENING

A term used to instruct you to create an opening in a line of stitching so the item may be turned right side out. The opening may be closed with *slip-stitching*, *tape fasteners*, or *zippers*.

OUTWARD

A term used to describe convex curves or corners that form an edge. See *Bias Binding*, *Hems*, and *Trims*.

PATTERN REPEATS

A term used to identify a design *motif* that is repeated at even intervals along the length of the fabric. This design element is an important feature when selecting fabric. The pattern repeat must be matched horizontally on each fabric width needed to make a pair of *curtains* or *draperies*, or *bedspread*, *couch cover*, or *shades*. When using a fabric with a repeating design, the length of the pattern repeat will affect the yardage requirements as each cut length will require the same number of pattern repeats. See *Bedspreads*, procedure #2 for fitted bedspread and yardage work sheet, procedure #10 for flat floor-length throw and coverlet work sheet; *Curtain and/or Drapery Yardage Work Sheet; Dust Ruffle* yardage work sheet; *Roman shade*, procedure #2, fabric yardage work sheet; *Tablecloths;* and *Walls*, procedure #2, measuring and yardage work sheet.

1. PLAN WHERE THE PREDOMINATE PORTION WILL FALL.

There are special visual considerations that must be evaluated before purchasing the fabric. For a fitted bedspread, have the pattern repeat go around the bed (A). For a flat bedspread, have the pattern repeat centered over the pillow (B). For a couch or chair, center the pattern repeat on the back rest and seat cushion (C). For curtains and draperies, have the bottom edge of the pattern repeat fall near the proposed hemline. If the whole pattern is not needed to make the total length, it will be lost in the gathers or pleats (D).

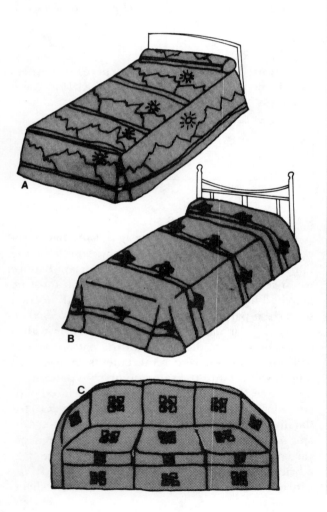

2. AT THE STORE,

you will need to measure the length of the pattern repeat and determine where the predominant motif will fall as explained above (A). Besides the yardage needed to complete your project, you must also determine where the first cut for the pattern repeat will be. Lay the fabric on the cutting table wrong side up and bring the selvages together, turning one edge under and matching the design for the full length of the pattern repeat (B). *Be aware* that the selvage edges often have less design and some areas will look the same. Have the salesperson mark where you plan the first cut with a strip of masking tape at each selvage or by using another method you both agree upon.

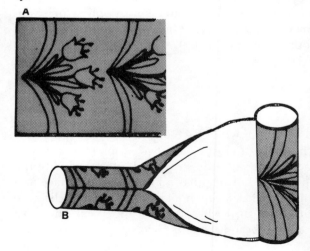

3. AT HOME, use one yardstick or two yardsticks taped together so you can draw a straight line across the fabric from selvage to selvage. On the right side draw a line with *tailor's chalk* crosswise between marks. Printed and solid-color fabrics must be used "as is" and cannot be straightened along a pulled thread, so follow the pattern design when drawing lines. You may also notice this along the selvage when matching the pattern repeats or making hems on a squared design. *Do not* purchase fabric that is extremely off-grain. Also see *Straightening Fabric Ends.*

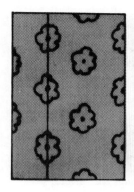

B

HINT: For all cuts, mark each pattern repeat by numbering it in the selvage with a soft lead pencil so it is easier to cut the correct length with the required number of pattern repeats.

4. JOINING FABRIC WIDTHS. When your project requires piecing, be sure the seams are placed for the most pleasing look. When matching pattern repeats for stitching, refer to *Basting,* using pin-basting procedure #3 or slip-basting procedure #4.

To join two widths for one panel to be used for a bedspread, comforter, Roman shade, or tablecloth, split one width in half. Stitch the smaller sections to each side of the full width, matching pattern repeats (A).

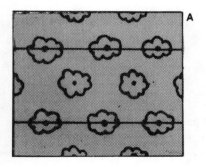

A

An uneven amount of fabric widths are sometimes needed for curtains and draperies to achieve the desired fullness. Have two or more full fabric widths for each panel meet at the center opening. Split the last width in half and stitch to the sides that will be next to the wall (B).

PICTURE FRAMING

A quick way to frame a fabric *motif* from yardage, a rug, towel, or your own needlework is to use an artist's stretcher frame. Purchase the correct width and length to accommodate your project.

1. MAKE A BORDER FOR SMALL DESIGNS, using contrasting or matching fabric. Cut the border fabric large enough to be stapled onto the stretcher frame. Using a ½″ seam allowance on the border fabric (and the same amount on the piece to be inserted), cut away the center. Reinforce each opening corner with small machine stitches ½″ from the cut edges. Clip corners to stitching (A). On the wrong side, turn down the opening edges ½″; press, being careful not to stretch the edges (B). Center border over your design and pin in place. Stitch border to design close to the pressed edges (C).

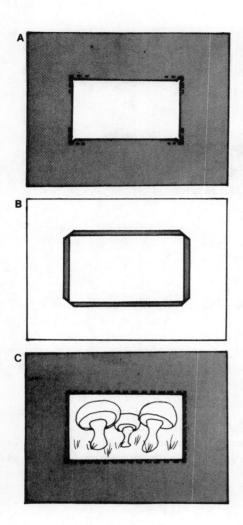

ners in the same manner. Make smooth folds at each corner, aligning the folds with the corners of the frame. Pull taut across the back and staple (C). Add a picture frame hanger or insert in a decorative frame to hang.

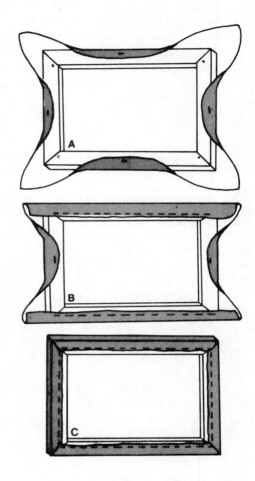

2. TO FRAME A FABRIC PICTURE with or without a bordered design, use the following steps: First assemble the frame and tack corners to hold securely. Now center the frame over the wrong side of the fabric. Place a staple at the center of each bar, stretching the fabric taut (A). Make sure the motif is centered, then staple the top, keeping the raw edge parallel to the inner frame edge. Work on each side of the center, ending about 1″ from the corners. Do the same for the bottom, making fabric taut (B). Staple sides to within 1″ of the cor-

PILLOW

Initially a pillow was a flat bag of feathers or wool used for a soft headrest. Today, pillows have been given a glamorous connotation by interior decorators who have taken the lowly bed pillow and used it to create colorful accents as well as backrests. See

Knife-edge Pillows with it's many variations, including quick-and-easy styles, harem corners, sunburst tops, and no-sew covers.

PILLOW SHAMS

Quite often pillow shams are used as a decorative cover for bed pillows, so think of them as a second pillowcase that is removed at night and replaced each morning when making the bed. Use this same method to make decorative throw pillows, eliminating the need for a hand-sewn or zipper closure.

Measure the pillow form as explained in *Knife-edge Pillows* for squares and rectangles.

For a self-ruffled, corded, or purchased trim edge, add 2" to each measurement (1" for easy removal and 1" for two ½" seam allowances).

For a flanged edge, add 6" or more to each measurement (4" for two 2" flanges, 1" for easy removal and 1" for two ½" seam allowances).

For both styles, make a pattern, then cut out the front. Divide the pattern in half between the narrowest edges. For a lapped closure on the pillow sham back, add 6" to this line. Cut out two pieces this size. Narrow hem the ends to be lapped (A).

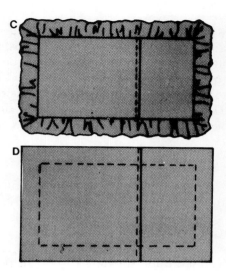

For a self-ruffle or other trim, baste trim to the front section and handle as one layer during construction.

For both styles, pin one back section to the front with right sides together, keeping raw edges even, and allowing the hemmed edge to fall beyond the center. Pin remaining back section to the opposite end, overlapping the hemmed edges to form closure. Stitch front to back in a ½" seam (B). Turn right side out through lapped opening; press edges flat (C).

For a flanged edge, stitch the desired measurement from the pressed outer edges (D), making sure the lapped closure is flat on the back.

PIN-BASTING
See *Basting,* procedure #3.

PINCH PLEATS
See *Draperies,* procedure #4, for self-pleated headings.

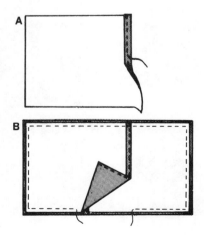

PINS

These small implements with a point at one end and a head at the other are used to fasten layers of fabric and trim temporarily. Pins should be fine enough to slip through the fabric easily and long enough to hold heavier fabric in place. Pins come in several lengths and thicknesses; each type should be matched to the fabric for each special project.

PIPING

Another term used for *cording,* piping is usually made with a tiny cord $1/16''$–$1/8''$ in diameter.

PIVOT

A directive used when stitching corners or points. To pivot, stitch to within $1/2''$–$5/8''$ of the next edge (or your seam allowance width); with needle still in fabric, raise the presser foot. Pivot (swing) fabric on needle so you can stitch the remaining edge along the same width seam line. Drop presser foot and continue stitching.

PLACE MATS

See *Napkins, Place Mats,* and *Table Runners.*

PLAIDS

Plaid fabric may have a printed or woven design and the bars should be matched at seam or for companion panels for a pair of curtains or drapes. See *Pattern Repeats.*

PLATFORM BED

See *Bed Lexicon,* style E.

PLASTIC SCREW ANCHORS

An aid used on hollow walls for lightweight objects. See *Anchor.*

PLEATER TAPE

A quick way to make pinch pleats on draperies and café curtains. To use, see *Draperies,* procedures #1 and #2.

PLEATS

These folds of definite, even widths are made by doubling the fabric on itself and then pressing it into sharp creases. Pleats have decorated home furnishings for centuries. They appear in many forms and the following styles are used throughout this book. See *Draperies,* procedure #4, to make self-pleated headings.

Box pleats are created with two folds that turn toward each other under the box. They may be used singly (A) or in a continuous strip (B).

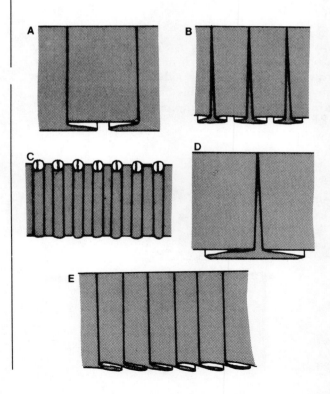

Cartridge pleats, which get their name from the cartridge belt used to hold extra ammunition, are used at the top of draperies and *valances* in place of the traditional pleats. These cylinder-shaped loops are open at the top and bottom and may need the support of a roll of heavy paper or cardboard to retain their shape (C).

Inverted pleats are usually found at corners. To make an inverted pleat, bring two creased edges together forming a doubled layer with a layer of fabric underneath the creases. The pleat folds may be as narrow as 1" or as deep as 6" on each side of the creased edges (D).

Knife pleats hang in long, slender folds 1"–2" wide and are a favorite for *bedspreads* and *dust ruffles.* A doubled layer of fabric is formed over another layer with the creases all going in the same direction (E).

Pinch pleats are used at the top of café curtains and draperies. See *Draperies,* procedure #2, for pinch pleats made with pleater tape, and procedure #4 for self-pleated pinch pleats.

PRESHRUNK FABRIC

Some decorator fabrics have "preshrunk" stamped on the selvage along with cleaning instructions. Be sure your fabric is washable. Many 100 percent cotton fabrics are treated with soil-release surfaces that may be lost when the fabric is washed. Some of the preshrunk fabrics may shrink even more if you do not follow the instructions printed on the selvage.

PRESS

A term used to direct a lift and press action instead of sliding the iron over the fabric.

PRIMARY COLORS

There are three pure colors: red, yellow, and blue. All shades and tints are produced from these three colors.

PRINTS

Most of the beautiful decorator fabrics are printed. Some of the all-over designs do not need to be matched but, most often, prints have a predominant motif that must be aligned and matched. See *Pattern Repeats.*

PRISCILLA CURTAINS

A long-time favorite with their ruffled edges and tiebacks, Priscilla curtains may meet at the center or be crisscrossed. This same style is now being made in lined decorator fabrics for *stationary draperies.* To create a one-of-a kind window treatment for your home, see *Curtains, Draperies, Ruffles,* and *Tiebacks.*

QUILTING BY MACHINE

Add a decorator touch to your favorite accessory by quilting a portion of your project or use a quilted design on one of the coordinating fabrics for a chair cushion, a pillow, or a bedspread top. Start with a small project and then work up to a patchwork quilt or bedspread throw. Patchwork can be a geometric design or one of the traditional designs. Use the seams as a quilting guide on smaller squares or add additional lines on the larger ones after the outlines are quilted. Use *bias binding* in the traditional manner to finish your quilt, throw, or chair pads.

Fabric selection is very important for quilting; use tightly woven light- or medium-weight fabrics such as decorator fabrics, calico, sheets, or any cotton blends. Be sure fabric for the backing has the same cleaning requirements as the quilt top. Use bonded polyester *batting.* A quilting foot attachment on your sewing machine will help keep the lines straighter. Use two fabric layers at least 3"–6" longer on all edges than the finished requirements. Fabric *shrinks* about 10 percent when the layers are quilted together over the batting. Purchase a sheet of polyester batting the same size as the cut measurement of the top fabric or slightly larger. Center fabric motifs both lengthwise and crosswise when cutting out the top. Piece layers as necessary; use one fabric width at the center of the top with piecing at each side and make a center seam for the backing so the seams do not fall in the same place. Trim selvages off after seams are stitched. Press seams open.

Decide what design will be quilted. Lines may be 6"–10" apart when quilting squares (A) or diamonds (B), and 5"–8" apart for lengthwise lines (C). You may want to quilt a motif printed on the fabric, using the stripes, plaid, floral, or geometric figures as a quilting pattern (D).

Before assembling, mark top with chalk or a soft lead pencil at even intervals. For squares, draw the first lines through the center of the fabric lengthwise and crosswise; for vertical lines, draw the line at the center of the top lengthwise; for diamonds, measure down each side the same distance as the top is wide so the diamonds are squared. Draw diagonal lines from corner to corner on each side. Fill in all lines as required for your quilting pattern. When using the fabric motif, no lines are needed.

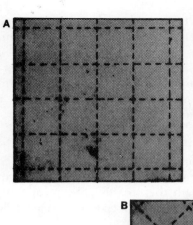

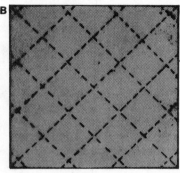

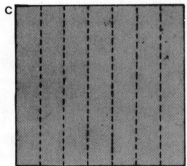

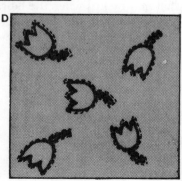

To assemble for quilting, work on a large flat surface such as a floor with wall-to-wall carpeting or a large rug. For those who do not have the space to spread the fabric and batting on the floor, make a frame with four C-clamps (purchased at a hardware store), four 1″ × 2″ boards at least 12″ longer than your fabric measurements, and a large quantity of push-pins. Make sure the frame is squared. Balance the frame on four chairbacks or other furniture of equal height while working.

When using carpet or rug, spread out the backing fabric, wrong side up; secure corners and edges using long pins inserted into the carpet. Lay batting over the back, keeping both layers smooth; secure with pins. Cover batting with the top, right side up; keep all three layers smooth and squared. Secure top over batting, removing pins used for the back as you work.

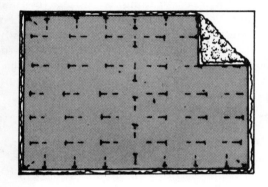

To pin-baste all three layers together for quilting, work from the center out both lengthwise and crosswise and insert pins straight down through all layers into the carpet, marking the top into quarters. Do one quarter at a time, pinning along your drawn lines or the seams and working out to the edges. When all intersecting lines are marked, start along one edge and slide a hand under the backing (next to the carpet) so a pin is between two fingers. With other hand, swing pin around to pin-baste all three layers together, keeping all layers wrinkle-free. Repeat this process with all pins until all areas you want to quilt are securely basted with pins.

When using a frame, place backing wrong side up and anchor in place with pushpins at 12″–14″ intervals. Lay a sheet of batting over the back, keeping the batting smooth and wrinkle-free without stretching; secure to frame and backing at corners and several other spots along each side. Trim batting edges even with backing edges if necessary. Cover batting with the top, right side up. Keeping all three layers smooth and squared, carefully secure all three layers to the frame, adding and/or removing pushpins as required.

HINT: When making a large quilted *throw,* it may be necessary to pin the back, batting, and top together along all four edges, and then roll all three layers on each narrow end in order to reach the centers. With all four corners of the frame supported, remove the C-clamps from one end. Roll up the fabric and batting on the board one-half the amount needed to reach the center for basting; reclamp boards together. Do the same for the opposite end. Pin-baste centers and quarters as required and unroll to complete basting.

For both methods, before quilting, test your sewing machine. Use 8–10 stitches to an inch and release the pressure on the presser foot slightly so the fabric and batting will move freely. For large pieces, quilt around the edges first, following your pattern. For fabric motifs, stitch around the design, then fill in with random lines so the spaces are no more than 10″ apart.

To quilt, make a larger work surface around your machine, using a cardtable or chairbacks to support the fabric so it won't pull or distort. Roll up quilting in a tight roll so it will go under the machine head. Spread fabric between your hands as you work to prevent puckers on both the top and backing.

When the quilting is completed, cut to required measurements and complete project as planned.

R

REINFORCEMENT STITCHES

A directive term indicating the need for a row of fine machine stitches (about 20 stitches to the inch) to be placed alongside the proposed seam line in the seam allowance of corners and curves. This layer of fabric may be clipped to the stitching, enabling the reinforced layer to be stitched to the opposite shaped corner or curve. When stitching the seam, stitch alongside the inner edge of the reinforcement stitches so they can't be seen from the outside when the fabric is turned right side out.

REMOVABLE COVERS

See *Bathrooms* for a sink skirt, *Bolster Covers, Box-edge Cushions, Duvet, Garment Bags, Headboards* for a slipcover, *Knife-edge Pillows, Pillow Sham.*

RETURN

The side or end parts of a curtain or drapery rod that extend from the wall to the front span. A curtain rod has the two returns shaped into a continuous piece with the front span. A drapery rod is designed to be hung with a return or a decorative bracket. The style with a return will hold the drapery next to the wall on both sides and across the front span; on the bracket style, the draperies are hung across the front span only.

REUPHOLSTERY

The simplest reupholstery project is recovering chair seats that do not require sewing because they have been covered with a square of fabric that has been stapled in place. See *Chair Cushions,* procedure #3.

REVERSE TUCK ROMAN SHADES

See *Roman Shades,* procedure #7.

ROD COVERS

There are many ways to cover wooden or PVC pipe rods for stationary draperies. Use paint in a matching or contrasting color or cover the rod in matching fabric.

For a gathered tubelike cover, with or without a heading, make the tube the same fullness as the draperies. For a plain gathered tube without a heading, cut a strip long enough for the desired fullness and as wide as the thickest part of the rod or elbow, plus 2″ (1¼″ for two ⅝″ seam allowances, ¾″ for ease). For a gathered tube with a heading, use the same measurements as for the plain tube for length and width, adding two times the desired finished heading height. Narrow hem ends; stitch long seam and turn right side out. For a cover with a heading, press tube flat along the seam only; stitch the two layers together the planned distance away, forming the heading. Place rod cover between drapery panels, distributing the fullness evenly.

To staple or glue fabric to rod for a smooth cover, cut fabric the length of the pole or pipe plus 2″, and as wide as the circumference, plus 1″. Turn under one long edge ½″; press. First, staple or glue the raw edge of fabric to the pole or pipe, then wrap and attach the folded edge over the first edge, making cover taut. Wrap and secure ends, clipping them so the fabric will be flat instead of folded.

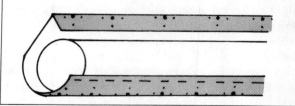

HINT: To make matching fabric-covered finials, take a circle of fabric and gather it over the finial, tying it at the tip and other grooves with matching thread. Pad with some *batting* and staple or glue the ends flat as for the rod.

ROD POCKET

A term sometimes used to describe the casing needed to hang a curtain or drapery. See *Casings.*

RODS

There are many styles of rods used to hang curtains and draperies. See *Curtain and/or Drapery Rods.*

ROLLER SHADES

These traditional window shades or blinds can help save energy when placed so the shade is next to the glass. There are several commercial products on the market that can be bonded to the wrong side of your fabric, or you can glue your fabric to a medium or heavy coated shadecloth or quality vinyl shade. Inexpensive plastic shades may not work as well as they have a tendency to stretch.

To cover a shade, decide how you want to finish the hem and use white fabric craft glue applied with a brush, spray craft fabric adhesive that dries clear, or liquid laundry starch applied directly from the bottle with a sponge. Remove the shade from the roller and wipe clean with a damp cloth, if necessary. Dry thoroughly and carefully remove stitches from the hem.

Work on a flat surface that can be wiped free of glue or starch. Tape fabric to surface wrong side up, keeping it squared and wrinkle-free. Roll up shade with the right side out. Start at the top of the shade and work toward the hem. Center shade over the predominant design motifs and tape top of shade in place after the glueing agent has been applied, making sure the entire surface of the fabric has been covered so you do not have dry spots that will show up as dull spots when the shade is completely dry. When drying is completed, carefully trim away excess fabric along the shade to retain the shade's original width.

Be aware that shades wider than the 54″ decorator fabric will create a handling problem unless the shade length requirement is no longer than this width (use fabric crosswise from selvage to selvage to eliminate the need for piecing). Fabric is not seamed; instead, the seam allowances are cut away and the cut edges are butted together over the shade during the glueing process. To match the *pattern repeat,* fold back the selvages and match the design; cut along the folds in a straight smooth line for butting.

Make a hem, using any of the following styles, for your fabric-covered roller shade:

To Make a Casing to Hold the Wooden Slat, use a plain or decorative style. For a plain style, turn up lower edge about 1¾″, or wide enough to accommodate the slat; stitch ¼″ from inner edge, using the longest machine stitch (A). Insert slat and attach a pull at the center of the shade if desired.

For a decorative edge, cut out a design, making a pattern first, allowing at least 3″ for a casing. To make a casing for the slat, fold bottom of shade wrong sides together the planned distance from the decorative edge. Stitch required distance from fold (B). Insert slat and pull down decorative edge. Decorative trim may be glued to the shaped edge (C).

To make a tab and rod hem, cut four or more tabs from matching fabric about 10″ long and 3″–6″ wide. Encase the long tab edge with *fold-over braid* (D). Fold tabs wrong sides together and place on wrong side of shade. Encase tab ends and shade bottom with fold-over braid. Insert rod through tab loops (E).

Attach roller to shade as planned, using staples or tacks; make sure it will hang straight and roll smoothly (F).

ROMAN SHADES

These beautiful fabric shades are currently replacing, or being used with, many traditional window treatments. Roman shades can be closed for privacy at night, and pulled up during the day into a colorful valance of soft folds to allow an unobstructed view. Not only do they add individualized charm to any room in your home, but also they can be made to conserve energy when made with insulated linings and hung flat against the glass or frame.

Roman shades may be hung from a board, a regular or café curtain rod, or a tension rod. The flat Roman shade allows you to show off a beautiful decorator fabric with a colorful design or a luxurious elegant one, and takes the least amount of fabric. As soon as you have mastered this simple style, you will want to make other versions such as the Reverse Tuck, procedure #7, Hobbled, procedure #8, or Loose Tuck with Eyelets, procedure #9, that vary only in length. The Balloon, procedure #10, and the Cloud, procedure #11, are made twice as wide as the Flat Roman Shade to create

these beauties. See *Austrian Shade* for sheer and lace fabrics that may be mounted the same as a Roman shade.

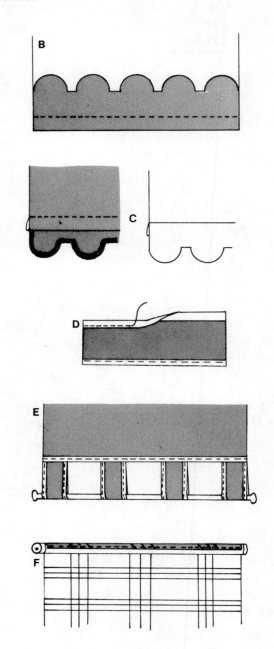

1. MEASURE WINDOWS. Carefully measure each window for shades, see *Measuring Windows.* There are two types of installation: next to the window or on the outside flat against the wall. To determine the finished shade size for each type of installation, standard measurements must be added to your finished width and length measurements in addition to the hem and mounting requirements.

For an indented installation, add ¾″ for every 36″ of width and length to your finished width and length measurements when making procedures #5 through #9 to allow for *shrinkage* after the rings or tape have been stitched in place.

For an outside installation, add at least 8″ to the finished width measurement for a 4″ extension on each side of the window and 4″ to the finished length measurement in order to mount the shade above the window on the wall or frame. Add 12″ more for a sliding glass door so the shade folds will stack above the door opening, and more length for a ceiling mount.

HINT: Many 54″-wide decorator fabrics are wide enough to be used crosswise from selvage to selvage for wider shades. Just be sure the design will look good sideways as this will eliminate seams.

2. ROMAN SHADE FABRIC YARDAGE WORKSHEET. Be sure to review procedure #1 above to help calculate yardage requirement, and procedure #4 below for additional fabric needs when mounting the shade and any additional fabric requirements for the style of shade selected.

To determine the number of fabric widths needed for each window, the following measurements are needed:

Window width		_____
Plus installation requirements	+	_____
Plus 3″ for side hems	+	3
Equals cut width for flat-style shades	=	_____

Style variations that require more width:

Balloon or Cloud shade window width		_____
Multiply 2, 2.5, 3 times width for fullness	×	_____
Equals actual cut shade width	=	_____
Austrian shade window width		_____
Multiply 1.3 times for fullness	×	1.3
Plus 8″ for cupping	+	8
Equals actual cut shade width	=	_____

For all styles, divide cut width   _____

    by fabric width: 36″, 44″, 48″, 54″, 60″   ÷ _____

Equals number of fabric widths   = _____

To determine the cut length of shade, the following measurements are needed. *Casings* for rods may need more than the 3″ allowed for mounting on a board:

Finished shade length   _____

    Plus 3″ for mounting and 5″ for hem   + 8

Equals cut length for flat styles   = _____

Style variations that require more length:

    #7 Reverse Tuck, add _____ number of tucks multiplied by ½″–1″   + _____

    #8 Hobbled Shade, add finished length measurement for a doubled length   + _____

    #9 Tucks with eyelet, add _____ number of tucks multiplied by 2″   + _____

    #10 Balloon or #11 Cloud Shade, add 30″ to retain pouff at bottom   + 30

    Austrian Shade, multiply finished length _____ by 2.5 for lightweights, 3 for sheers   + _____

Equals style variation cut length   = _____

    For fabric with pattern repeat:

    Divide cut length by pattern *repeat* length   ÷ _____

    Equals number of repeats per length. If fraction remains, round up to next full number   = _____

    Multiply by length of repeat   × _____

    Equals adjusted cut length   = _____

For all styles, multiply your cut length   _____

Times the number of fabric widths   × _____

Equals yardage in inches for shade   = _____

Add measurement to cover mounting board, if necessary   + _____

Equals adjusted length   = _____

Divided by 36   ÷ 36

Equals total yardage for each shade   = _____

Lining Yardage Requirements		
Actual shade cut width		_____
Less 3″ for side hems	−	3
Equals adjusted cut lining width	=	_____
Divided by lining width 48″, 54″	÷	_____
Equals number of lining widths	=	_____
Cut shade length		_____
Less amount needed for hem	−	5
Equals cut lining length	=	_____
Multiply by number of fabric widths	×	_____
Equals yardage in inches	=	_____
Add 4″ for weight rod if necessary	+	_____
Equals adjusted yardage in inches	=	_____
Divided by 36	÷	36
Equals total yardage for each shade	=	_____

HINT: The mulitlayered lining must be pieced at the selvages. Use your adjusted cut lining width measurement, purchasing two or more strips this long to be seamed together to equal your lining measurement. Linings that have an insulation bonded to them *do not* need special consideration.

3. NOTIONS, LUMBER, AND HARDWARE FOR SHADES. Notion requirements for rings, shade tape, eyelets, and cord will vary according to style.

For mounting, use a thin board ½″–1″ thick and 1″–3″ wide, or the desired curtain rod.

Hardware needed: ⅜″ metal rod to be used as a weight to hold shade flat and about ½″ shorter than your finished width measurement; screw eyes large enough to hold all cords, plus one more to hold cords next to wall (for extra-wide windows or very long shades, tiny pulleys work more easily); awning cleat; 2 or more *angle irons* with screws for hanging board.

HINT: When hanging a curtain rod on the wall, you will also need a board to anchor the screw eyes for the cord. Paint board to match the wall if you do not wish to wrap it with fabric. For an indented installation, use the top of the window opening to anchor the screw eyes when using a rod.

To use rings instead of Roman shade tape, use the finished shade length divided by number of horizontal rows (rings may be 5″–12″ apart; 6″ is the favorite to make narrower folds), which equals the number of rings per vertical row. __ ÷ __ = __ Times the number of vertical rows (spaces between rows can be 10″ for heavyweight fabric and/or lining to 30″ for a #11 Cloud shade made with sheer fabric. __ × __ = __, the total number of rings needed for each shade.

Yardage Work Sheet for Shade Tape

Austrian shades require Austrian shade shirr-tape with rings. Roman shade tape is required for the Flat Roman Shade (unlined) #6 and the Hobbled Shade #8 and it may be used for procedures #5, #10, and #11, if desired, or substitute rings.

For Austrian shades and Roman shades

Use cut length measurement   _____

Times number of vertical rows required   × _____

Equals yardage in inches   = _____

Plus one extra ring for each vertical row _____ to align rings
    horizontally × space measurement between rings   + _____

Equals required inches   = _____

Divided by 36   ÷ ____36____

Equals total yards of tape per shade   = _____

Yardage Work Sheet for Cord

Use durable nylon cord found in hardware stores.
Finished shade length   _____

Times number of vertical rows _____ of rings or eyelets, plus 1   × _____

Equals inches for length   = _____

Plus width measurement _____ × vertical rows _____, less 1   + _____

Equals total yardage in inches   = _____

Divided by 36   ÷ ____36____

Equals total yards of cord per shade   = _____

4. MOUNTING FINISHED SHADE: Follow this sequence of directions to mount your shade:

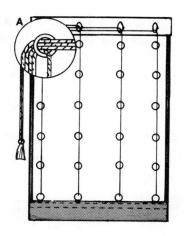

To cover the weight rod, cut a 4″ wide strip of lining or matching fabric (if lining is not used) the length of the rod plus 2″. Wrap and glue in place, tucking in the raw ends, or make a tube by stitching the long edges together. Turn tube right side out; insert rod, tucking in ends, and *tack* in place.

To cover mounting board, use a strip of the shade fabric the length of the board plus 2″–4″ and the circumference plus 1″. Wrap board and lap cut edges on top, tucking in the ends to cover the raw edges. Staple or glue fabric in place or paint to match wall. Attach *angle iron* brackets as directed below, if required, but *do not* hang permanently. Hang curtain rods if being used.

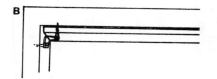

Staple shade to top of board, placing stitched upper edge even with back edge that will be even with wall or window. Mark position for screw eyes at each end of the vertical rows of tape or rings and anchor.

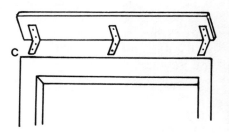

Attach cords: Cut cord and knot securely to the bottom of each vertical row of rings or eyelets, threading cord up through remaining rings or eyelets on each vertical row. Thread cord through corresponding screw eye and continue across the top through the screw eyes to the side that will be the right-hand side when the shade is hung, continuing down to the hem. To prevent raveling, hold cord over a securely placed candle. Keeping cord taut, melt cord apart. Lightly knot cords together (A).

For an indented installation, fasten angle irons to the ends of the mounting board and secure to the sides of the window frame (B) or hang shade on curtain rod and put screw eyes in place.

For an outside installation, fasten angle irons to the back of the mounting board and secure board to window frame or wall (C). Hang curtain rod with mounting board underneath, allowing enough space for the shade.

The awning cleat should be anchored at a comfortable spot on the right side of the window. Test to make sure all cords pull evenly and knot near the top. Braid cords together so they wrap around the cleat more easily.

5. FLAT ROMAN SHADE (LINED):

This is the easiest shade to make (A). All other styles are variations of this method with the exception of the *Austrian* or *roller shade*. To finish this shade, add 3″ to the shade fabric width measurement for two side hems and 8″ (3″ for mounting, 5″ for hem) to the length measurement. Make lining 3″ narrower and 5″ shorter than the shade fabric.

Carefully measure your windows, see *Measuring Windows*. Review procedure #4 for additional fabric requirements. Calculate yardage for fabric and lining, using procedure #2; then purchase notions, lumber, and hardware, following procedure #3. Rings are recommended for all lined shades.

To join lining to fabric, cut and seam fabric and lining as required for your shade. The lining will be 3″ narrower and 5″ shorter than the shade fabric. With right sides together and upper edges even, pin lining to fabric at both side edges; stitch together in ¾″ seams (B). Turn right side out; center lining over shade with upper edges even. Turn seam allowances toward side edges; press flat. Machine-baste or zigzag top edges together (C).

To make hem, using weight rod, turn in top edge 3″ and bottom edge 2″; press. Stitch 1¼″ from bottom fold, forming a casing for rod (D). Turn up stitched lower edge 3″; press. Stitch close to inner folded edge to hold hem in place. Insert rod in pocket and *slipstitch* ends together. Or stitch ends and hem in place in one continuous stitching, starting and ending at lower edge (E).

Attach rings: The placement for both the horizontal and vertical rows of rings should have been worked out at the time of purchase as explained in procedure #3 above. Place shade on a flat surface so the shade fabric and lining will be smooth and wrinkle-free. A vertical row of rings is placed at each side hem seam. Draw a line with chalk at even intervals across the shade between the side hem seams. Pin shade fabric and lining together along side hems and marked vertical lines. Mark position for horizontal rows, placing the first row at the inner hem edge. Attach rings by hand or machine through both layers as the shade will not fold correctly if fabric and lining are not attached at each ring. When sewing rings by hand, use thread that matches the shade fabric. When zigzagging the rings in place by machine, use thread that matches the shade on the bobbin and thread that matches the rings on top. Use a large pin under the ring, zigzagging over both ring and pin for a more flexible anchor (F). Following procedure #4 above, mount shade as planned.

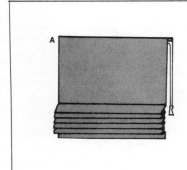

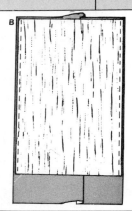

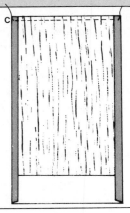

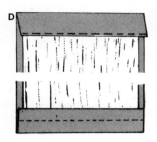

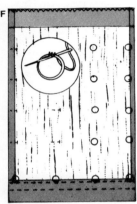

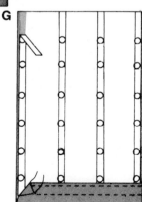

6. FLAT ROMAN SHADE (UNLINED).

Use sheer or lightweight fabrics that will not fade. When using more than one fabric width, plan seams so they will fall over a tape, pressing seams open. To finish this shade, add 3″ to the width measurement for two side hems and 8″ (3″ for mounting, 5″ for hem) to the length measurement.

Carefully measure your windows, see *Measuring Windows.* Review procedure #4 for additional fabric requirements. Calculate yardage, using procedure #2; purchase notions, lumber, and hardware, following procedure #3. Roman shade tape is required for this style of construction.

To prepare side hems and top, first seam fabric to required width. Turn in side edges 1½″; press. Turn down top edge 3″; press. Or, prepare *casing,* pressing and only pinning it in place.

Prepare bottom hem at this time same as for procedure #5 above, steps C and D, but *do not* insert rod or stitch hem at this time.

To apply Roman shade tape, place strip of tape over one side edge, placing tape end under the bottom hem so the first ring will start at hem edge (G). Cut all tapes to this measurement, making sure rings are at the same position horizontally for each strip.

Pin tapes to the side pressed edges so the raw edges are enclosed; stitch both long edges to shade through all thicknesses, using thread that matches the shade fabric on the bobbin and thread on top that matches the tape. Divide remaining width equally between tapes needed and stitch in place in the same manner, keeping rings lined up horizontally across all shade tapes.

Complete hem stitching for weight rod or stitch casing in place if being used. Follow procedure #4 to mount shade.

7. REVERSED TUCK SHADE. This structured Roman shade folds flat and compact each time it is raised (A). Spaces between tucks may be as narrow as 2″ for small windows and as wide as 6″ for large windows. A ⅛″-thick wire or dowel is used in the front tucks to prevent sagging. For most fabrics, use a ¼″ deep tuck; heavier fabrics may need tucks ⅜″–½″ deep. To finish this shade, add the same measurements used for procedure #5, plus the additional amount needed for tucks to the length.

Carefully measure your windows, see *Measuring Windows.* Review procedure #4 for additional fabric requirements.

To calculate yardage use procedure #2 above, after you decide how wide the spaces and tucks should be: Take the finished length measurement __, less 3″ (hem area) __−3 = __ divide by space depth ÷ __; equals number of rows of tucks = __, times tuck allowance (½″–1″) × __, equals additional style length required = __. Example: For a finished length of 30″ with 2″ spaces and ¼″ tucks, dividing 27″ by 2″ equals 13 spaces, plus 1″. Since you need an equal number of spaces for tucks, use 12 spaces and tucks, having 3″ extra at the top without a tuck. Multiply ½″ tuck requirement times 12, equals 6″ additional fabric required.

Carefully calculate yardage using procedure #2 and purchase notions, lumber, and hardware following procedure #3. Rings must be used for this style.

To prepare shade for tucks, cut and seam fabric and lining as required for your shade following Flat Roman Shade, procedure #5, steps A through D above.

To make tucks, start at the hem end. From the lining side, measure up ¼″, or the measurement of the tuck. Make fold at this point across the shade, matching side edges; pin, making sure the space between fold and hem is equal. Stitch a scant ¼″–½″ from fold, *back-stitching* at each end to form

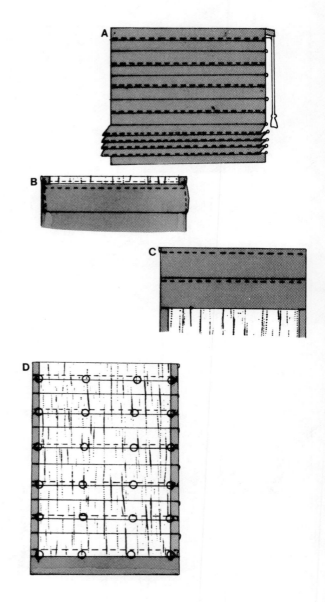

tuck (B). From the shade side, measure up 2¼″, or the measurement of the space plus the width of the tuck. Stitch a scant ¼″–½″ from fold (C). Repeat this process, reversing tucks from front to back of shade until all tucks are stitched. Attach vertical rows of rings to tucks on the lining side (D). On the shade side, insert wires or dowels into tucks. Follow procedure #4 to mount shade.

8. HOBBLED SHADE. A favorite, with soft horizontal pleats when the shade is down. Be sure to consider the stacking when the shade is pulled up to the top of the window (A). Shades may need to be placed higher to accommodate the extra stacking. To finish this shade, add the same measurements used for procedure #5, plus twice the finished length measurement for the horizontal folds.

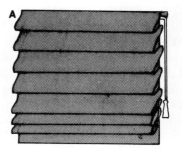

Carefully measure windows, see *Measuring Windows.* Review procedure #4 for additional fabric requirements. Calculate yardage for fabric and lining using procedure #2, and purchase notions, lumber, and hardware following procedure #3. Roman shade tape is required for hobbled shades; you may substitute twill tape and rings, if desired.

To prepare shade, cut and seam fabric and lining as required for shade, following Flat Roman Shade #5, steps A through D above, but *do not* insert rod and stitch hem at this time.

To mark shade for hobbled horizontal pleats, work from the lining side. Measure up from the bottom edge the distance between the rings on the tape or 6"; mark with pins on each side through all thicknesses and divide the remaining width equally for remainder of tapes. Now make horizontal rows of pins twice the distance between the rings, or 12" apart, to the top of the shade, establishing the required number of vertical rows for tape (B).

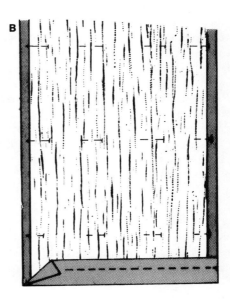

Cut Roman shade tape the finished length requirement of the shade, making sure there is enough tape below the first ring to tuck under the hem and to line up the rings horizontally on all tapes.

To attach tape to form hobbled pleats, place tapes over the vertical rows of pins, tucking tape ends under the unstitched hem. Place a ring over each pin and zigzag stitch over ring through all thicknesses, repeating this step at all pins (C). Insert weight rod and stitch hem in place. Complete shade, following procedure #4. On the shade side, excess fabric will drop down horizontally over each line of rings.

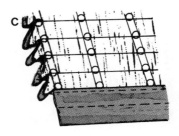

9. TUCKS WITH EYELETS SHADE.

This style of Roman shade has tucks 1" wide and 1" deep between unstitched folds. It is attractive with 2"-deep spaces and 4"-wide unstitched folds on small windows in plain dyed fabric, and up to 6"-deep spaces with up to 12" unstitched folds for other fabrics. To finish this shade, add the same measurements as for procedure #5 above, plus the additional amount needed for tucks to the length (A).

Carefully measure windows, see *Measuring Windows*. Review procedure #4 for additional fabric requirements. Purchase notions, lumber, and hardware following procedure #3. Eyelets (shower curtain or belt size) are used in place of rings.

To calculate yardage use procedure #2 above, after you decide how deep the spaces will be: Take the finished length measurement less 3" (hem area) __, divide by space depth __, equals number of rows of tucks __, times the 2" tuck allowance __, equals additional length required for this style __. Example: For a 40" finished shade length with 6" spaces, divide 37" by 6" equals 6 spaces plus 1" and 6 tucks, adding a tuck to top of hem equals 7 tucks. Multiply 2" times the 7 tucks equals 14" additional fabric required. Calculate yardage for fabric and lining, using procedure #2.

To prepare shade, cut and seam fabric and lining as for Flat Roman Shade procedure #5, steps A through D above.

To make tucks, start at hem edge on the lining side. Measure up 1", making a fold at this point across the shade; pin, making sure measurement is equal and the side edges are lined up. Starting at one side, stitch a scant 1" from the fold for 1", *back-stitching* at each end of the stitching. Do the same for the other side. Divide remaining width equally between the 1"-wide stitching for tucks. Measure up 7" for a 6" space and 1" tuck, or desired depth plus 1". Make and stitch remaining tucks as planned (B).

To complete shade, attach eyelets opposite each stitched tuck according to package instructions. Tie cord to bottom eyelets and thread through remaining rows of eyelets the same as for rings; complete shade following procedure #4.

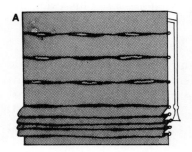

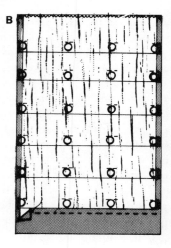

10. BALLOON SHADE.

This vertical, pleated Roman shade beauty is used with every style of decorating and is often used as a valance in a shorter length (A). Make this shade so it hangs straight on the sill or remains slightly pouffed. To finish this shade, add 3" (two 1½" side hems) and double the finished width for the total width measurement and 4½" (3" for mounting, 1½" for hem) to the length measurement. Lining is 3" narrower and 1½" shorter.

Carefully measure your windows, see *Measuring Windows.* Calculate yardage for fabric and lining using procedure #2, and purchase notions, lumber, and hardware following procedure #3. Rings are recommended for this style.

When joining fabric widths, try to have the seams fall on the inside of a pleat fold. To check where seams may fall, use a strip of paper twice the finished width measurement. Make pleats as shown below, arranging seams accordingly, and adjust spaces between pleats where necessary.

To prepare shade, cut and seam fabric and lining as for Flat Roman Shades, procedure #5, steps A and B. Turn up lower edge 1½" over lining; press. Turn in raw edge to meet fold and stitch hem in place through all thicknesses (B).

To make pleats, divide extra fabric into pleats of equal size making *Inverted Pleat,* allowing at least 10" for each pleat. Make one half of an inverted pleat at each side and divide spaces equally between each pleat used (C). Pin and press pleats the full length of shade. To make pleats lie flatter, stitch ⅛" from inner pleat folds through fabric and lining, keeping front free of stitching.

Attach Weight Rod: Cover weight rod with lining fabric following procedure #4. Make doubled loops of lining fabric large enough to slip covered rod through and *tack* loops just above the hem at the sides and the center of each pleat. Place a ring over top edge of each loop and make vertical rows of rings at these places, keeping rings lined up horizontally. Insert rod through loops and tack loop to rod cover (D). To form permanent scallops at the bottom of the shade as planned, thread each cord through the bottom rings and five other rings in each corresponding vertical row, tying rings loosely together. Thread cords through remaining vertical rings; mount as planned following procedure #4 above.

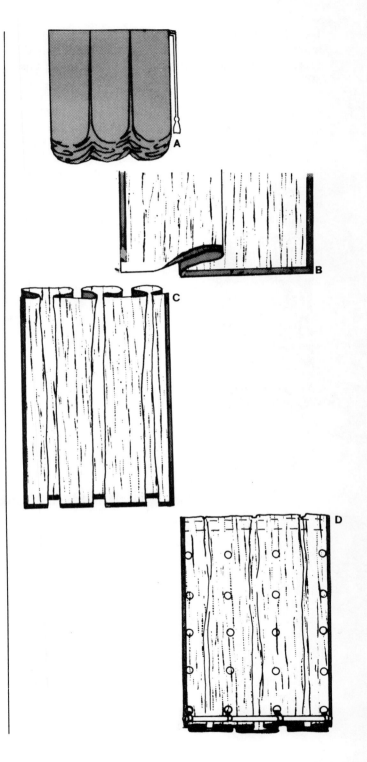

11. CLOUD SHADE: This soft fluffy shade may have wide or narrow scallops when pulled. Place vertical rows as close as 12″ or as far apart as 30″ with horizontal rows 6″ or less for smaller folds. There are two ways to finish the top of a cloud shade and three ways to finish the bottom. The top can be shirred with 4-cord shirr-tape and mounted on a board (A), or gathered on a curtain rod with a *casing* (B). The bottom can be finished with a plain hem, casing, or ruffles. This style of Roman shade should be lined when using decorator fabrics. To line, see Balloon Shade, procedure #10, step B above. For sheers, finish shade side hems and top as for *Curtains,* procedures #1 and #2. Rings are recommended for this style.

Carefully measure windows, see *Measuring Windows,* and review procedure #4 for additional fabric requirements. Select the top and bottom finishes from those suggested above, following the detailed methods below. Calculate yardage for fabric and lining using procedure #2; purchase notions, lumber, and hardware following procedure #3. Rings are recommended for this style.

Top with 4-cord shirr-tape, adding 6″ to the length requirement for a 1½″ heading and mounting. Purchase 4-cord shirr-tape the same measurement as your cut width. Prepare shade as planned. Add two rows of gathering thread at the top edge instead of basting for mounting. Use a mounting board.

To apply shirr-tape, place tape 6″ from top edge of shade and follow *Draperies,* procedure #10, for shirred heading, steps A and B, disregarding reference to casing. Turn shade top down 1½″ above the top row of stitching; pin. Stitch along the top row of stitching, forming a heading (C). Pull up cords and gathering threads to fit mounting board; distribute fullness along the cords. After board has been covered, staple shade to board, making gathers as smooth as possible, and mount shade following procedure #4 (D).

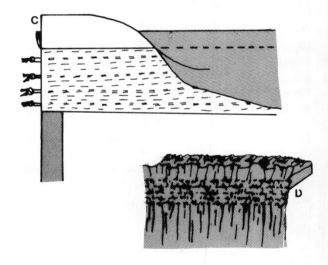

Top gathered on rod, use a *casing* with a heading, procedure #2. Make the heading ¼″–2″ for most rods.

Plain Hem, make the same as for *Balloon Shade,* procedure #10, step A, and attach weight rod with loops as in step D above; place loops at each end of the vertical rows of rings, just above the hem (after placing rings on the side edges, divide remaining width equally for vertical rows of rings that will form pouffed scallops).

Casing Hem: Adapt the hem allowance so *casing* will accommodate the weight rod. Turn in the raw edge ½″ and place ½″ over the lining (when being used); stitch casing in place.

Fasten as many vertical rows of rings as needed to form the desired amount of pouffed scallops (after placing a row of rings on each side hem), placing the first horizontal row on the fold of the casing. Start the next horizontal row 5″–6″ above the bottom of the casing.

Cover weight rod with lining or shade fabric. Insert rod into casing and *slip-stitch* ends shut. Distribute fullness evenly over the rod, having all vertical rows straight from top to bottom, and *tack* casing to rod cover at bottom of rod (E). To form permanent scallops at the bottom of the shade as planned, thread cord through the bottom rings and five more rings at each vertical row, tying rings loosely together. Thread cords through remaining vertical rings; mount as planned following procedure #4 above.

For a ruffled hem, adjust shade length to allow for the depth of the ruffle (a 3″ double-thickness ruffle cut from a 7″ wide strip of self-fabric makes an elegant finish). Use *Ruffles,* procedure #2 or #3 for an unlined Cloud Shade, and procedure #5 for the lined version, making lining the same length as the shade fabric.

Attach rings to shade as in procedure #5 for the Flat Roman Shade (lined), step F, starting first horizontal row at the ruffle seam and the second row the predetermined amount above the ruffled seam.

Cover weight rod with lining or shade fabric. Make fabric loops (which match the weight rod cover) large enough to slip covered rod through; *tack* loops on ruffled seam at each end of the vertical rows of rings. Insert rod through loops, tacking end loops near ends of rod cover as shown. Divide remaining loops evenly along rod; tack in place (F). To form permanent scallops at the bottom of shade

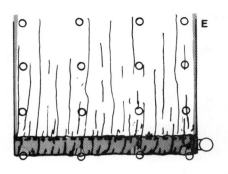

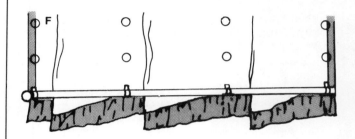

as planned, tie cords around each loop and through five rings on each vertical row, tying loop and rings loosely together. Thread cords through remaining vertical rings. For an unscalloped, straight hem, tie cord around loops and thread through rings. Mount as planned following procedure #4.

RUFFLES

Any narrow strip of fabric or trim that can be gathered along one edge can be made into a ruffle. There are four ways ruffles are used in decorating: applied to a hem edge; applied to a surface for an added dimension; enclosed with self-fabric for a hem edge; or stitched in a seam. Whether you use purchased ruffles or make your own in self- or contrasting fabric, the application is the same. Ruffles may be 1½ to 2 times the edge or surface where it will be stitched. Some medium to heavyweight fabrics look best at 1½ fullness while most other fabrics need the double fullness.

1. FORMING RUFFLE STRIPS.
Ruffles may be cut on the bias or straight grain and may be made of a single thickness or double thickness of fabric.

To make single-thickness ruffles, add 1″ to the desired finished width (½″ for seam allowance, ½″ for narrow hem) for a plain ruffle. For a ruffle with a heading or a double ruffle, add 1″ for two ½″ narrow hem allowances to the desired width.

When using the single-thickness ruffle, *clean-finish* any seams used for piecing or joining. For a continuous strip around a pillow or tablecloth, join ends in a seam and narrow hem one or both long edges (A). For a *Bedspread* or *Dust Ruffle,* narrow hem each end (B)

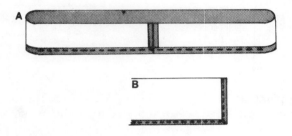

To make double-thickness ruffles, double the desired finished width. For a plain ruffle, add 1″ for two ½″ seam allowances. A ruffle with a heading or double ruffle does not need seam allowances.

When using the double-thickness ruffle, press seams open. For a continuous strip, stitch and press seams. Then fold in half, wrong sides together; press (A). Or stitch ends in a ¼″ seam and press as for the continuous strip (B).

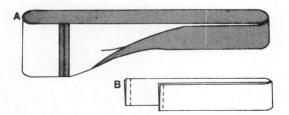

Add gathering threads as shown for each type of ruffle. For more direction, see *Gathers.*

2. APPLYING A RUFFLE AS A HEM FINISH.
The most familiar decorator touch with an applied ruffled hem is *Priscilla curtains.* Their ruffles may have a heading or be a double ruffle and may be a single or double thickness.

Use a ½″ hem allowance for this applied version. To prepare hem edge, fold up hem allowance ⅜″, right sides together; press.

For a ruffle with a heading, in a single thickness, narrow hem both long edges and add gathering threads about ½″ from the top. For a double thickness, fold one long edge to the wrong side ⅝″; press. Fold remaining long edge up to meet narrow edge; press. Add gathering threads ⅛″ from each raw edge. Narrow hem ends or join in a continuous strip as explained above (A).

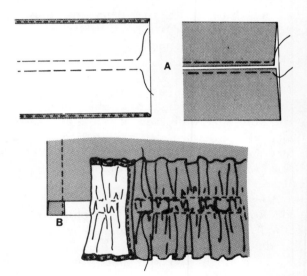

Pin ruffle over raw edge with fold ⅛″ below lower gathering threads. Adjust gathers; distribute evenly, allowing extra fullness at corners so ruffle will not cup when it extends beyond the edge. Stitch ruffle in place along both gathering threads as shown (B).

For a double ruffle, use a crisp fabric so the top ruffle will stand up. For a single thickness, narrow hem both long edges and add gathering threads at the center. For a double thickness, fold long edges to the wrong side so they meet at the center; press. Add gathering threads ⅛″ from each raw edge (A). Stitch the double ruffle to the hem edge as for ruffle with a heading, step B above (B).

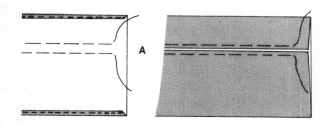

3. ENCLOSED HEM EDGE RUFFLE.

Use this plain ruffle on the bottom of a *cloud Roman shade, tablecloth,* or *bedspread.* A 1″ hem allowance is needed to enclose the raw ruffle edge. Be sure to subtract the finished width of the ruffle from the overall finished length of the item to be ruffled. Prepare ruffle strip as directed in procedure #1 for a plain ruffle, using a continuous strip or a finished end (A).

Pin ruffle in place so the raw edge is ½″ below the edge to be finished. Adjust gathers and distribute evenly. Stitch along inner gathering thread. Press seam allowance flat. Trim ruffle seam allowance only to a scant ¼″. Turn in raw hem allowance edge, then turn the folded edge down, encasing raw ruffle edge. Stitch inner edge in place (B). Turn ruffle down; press. On the outside, stitch ⅛″ from seam, catching enclosed ruffle seam on the stitching (C).

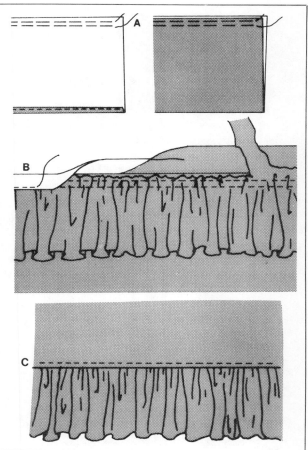

4. APPLYING RUFFLE TO A SURFACE. Add a touch of elegance to your favorite accent piece with an applied ruffle above a hem, around a pillow top, or below a casing on a ruffled curtain or stationary drapery. Prepare ruffle strips as directed in procedure #1 above.

For a plain ruffle, use a strip of *trim* to cover the raw edges. Pin prepared ruffle strips in place and gather to fit. Distribute gathers evenly; baste. Press seam allowances with tip of iron *only*. If necessary, trim seam allowance only to acommodate the band trim width. Place band trim over raw edges with its lower edge covering the gathering threads. Stitch both edges in place through all thicknesses (A).

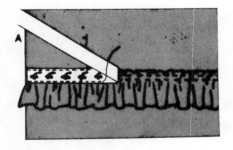

For a ruffle with a heading(B), or a double ruffle(C), place gathering threads as shown in procedure #2. Pin prepared ruffle strip in place and gather to fit. Distribute gathers evenly; baste. Stitch ruffle in place alongside both rows of gathering threads.

5. RUFFLES STITCHED IN A SEAM. Use this plain ruffle treatment at the side and hem edges of lined-to-edge Flat-Style *Bedspread,* procedure #12, or Stationary Draperies (see *Draperies,* procedure #8), *Knife-edge Pillow, Pillow Sham,* or a lined *Valance.* Prepare ruffle strip as directed in procedure #1 above.

For a continuous ruffle, divide strip into quarters and then eighths for long edges; mark with pins. Add gathering threads, breaking stitches at pins. Divide perimeter of squares or rectangles and circumference of circles with the same amount of pins. Pin ruffle to right side of fabric, matching pins (A). Adjust gathers to fit evenly, allowing extra fullness at corners so the ruffle does not cup. Baste ruffle in place alongside inner gathering threads. Press gathered edge of seam allowance only (B).

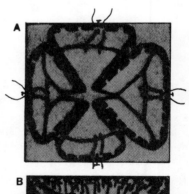

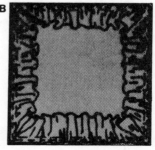

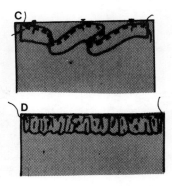

For a ruffle with finished ends, divide ruffle in halves, quarters, or eighths; mark with pins. Add gathering threads to raw edge, breaking stitches at pins, if necessary. Mark seam allowances at ends and divide remaining width with same number of pins. Pin ruffle in place, matching pins (C). Baste ruffle in place (D) and stitch seam as instructed above for step B.

To complete both types: after ruffle has been basted in place, place ruffled section over remaining section, right sides together and raw edges even; pin. Stitch together alongside the inner edge of the basting, leaving an opening for turning, if necessary.

SASH CURTAINS

These are used on the lower half of a double-hung window for privacy. The top of the curtain should be even with the top of the sash and end at the sill or apron. A sash curtain may be placed next to the glass or on the outside, anchored to trim or wall. Make the same as *Curtains,* procedure #1, for straight curtains, or substitute a Café Curtain, procedure #2, or Casement Curtains, procedure #3.

SCREENS

Use a one-section screen at your windows to help prevent heat loss; use a double- or triple-fold screen to frame your windows, or as a focal point, or as a divider, or to hide a structural flaw. For some uses, you may want to purchase a screen frame and install *casement curtains,* or use an inexpensive cardboard or fiberboard ready-made screen and glue on fabric to match your decor. When a specific size is needed, make your own—screens are quite easy to make, but they may be time-consuming.

Assemble Materials:
Frames should be 12″–18″ wide and as long as needed. Some screens need one center support while others that reach from floor to ceiling will need three or more center supports.

Lumber: For each panel that will make up your screen, use two 1″ × 2″ wood strips the length the screen will be; two 1″ × 2″ wood strips for the top and bottom of rectangle (to be placed between the long strips and long enough to make the frame as wide as needed), adding one or more center supports the same length.

Supplies: Corrugated nails; wood glue; staples, tacks, or glue gun and glue stick; decorative upholstery tacks; ½″-wide masking tape or tack strips.

Fabric: Flannel or an old white sheet to pad both sides of each panel; decorative fabric (be sure to consider *pattern repeat* when calculating yardage); for fabric hinges, 6″-wide strips of matching fabric the length of panel, plus 2″; or 3″-wide grosgrain ribbon this length; or use metal hinges.

Frame Construction: Apply glue to both surfaces before nailing frame together. With corners square, and edges butted tight together and in alignment, fasten joinings with corrugated nails. Do the same for center support(s). Allow glue to dry at least 24 hours.

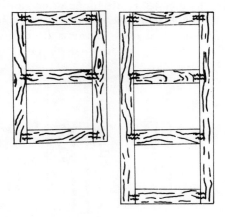

Pad with Flannel: For each panel, cut one flannel section its width and depth, adding 3″ to all edges and one flannel section 1″ smaller than its width and depth. Center frame over larger section, and wrap flannel around to the other side of the frame. Starting at the center of each edge, work to each corner, keeping fabric taut across the frame. Secure top first at inner edge of frame and do each side. *Miter* corners, making fabric smooth, and do the same for the bottom (A). Center smaller section over the uncovered side and secure over the raw edges of the first section (B).

Decorating Covering and Fabric Hinges. For each panel, cut one fabric section for the front its width and length, plus 2½″ on all edges, and one smaller

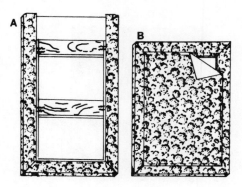

fabric section for the back ½″ larger than the panel on all edges. For fabric hinges, cut strips 6″ wide the length of panel, plus 2″.

To cover screen front: Center panel over the wrong side of the larger section with the stapled back of the padding facing you. Work from the top to the sides and then to the bottom the same way as for the padding. Pull fabric taut across the front without distorting the design (A).

For fabric hinges, fold strip in half lengthwise, wrong sides together, and tuck in the ends 1″; press. Place one-half of hinge strip on back of panel with top and bottom edges even; staple (B). If using grosgrain ribbon, turn in the raw ends before pressing and attach the same way. Attach metal hinges after the panels are completed.

To cover screen back, use masking tape or tack strips on the wrong side of each edge of the smaller sections, keeping corners free of tape (C). Turn in edges a scant ⅝″, mitering each corner (D). Center panel section over panel back, with right side up and folded edges about 1/16″ from outer edges. Fasten with decorative tacks, keeping fabric taut and making sure its edges cannot be seen from the front (E). Make another panel in the same way, aligning the panels to attach the fabric hinge before the back is tacked in place (F).

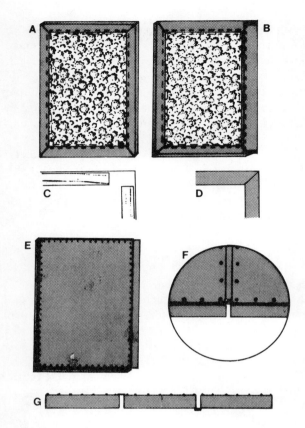

Plain seams: Used to stitch two layers together and then pressed open or pressed to one side. Sometimes the seam allowances must be *clean-finished* to prevent raveling.

Enclosed seams: To form a finished edge in place of a hem. After the seam is stitched, *trim, clip,* and/or *notch* seam allowances. Turn right side out, forming an edge along the stitching; press. Enclosed seam edges may be *edge-stitched* or *top-stitched.*

French seams: Used most often for sheer *curtains* and *draperies* when more than one fabric width is needed for each panel. Since selvages must be trimmed off to prevent puckered seams, the cut edges must be enclosed with fabric to prevent fraying. To make a French seam, place two fabric widths wrong sides together; pin. Stitch together in a ¼″ seam. Turn fabric along the row of stitching so the right sides of the fabric are together; press and then pin the two layers together so they will not shift when stitching. Stitch ⅜″ from the pressed edge, enclosing the cut edges. To make a mock French seam, see *Clean-finish,* step D.

To insert a decorative edging in a seam, see *Cording,* procedure #3; *Ruffles,* procedure #5; *Trims,* procedure #3.

Screens with Three or More Panels: Two front-panel sections must be adapted to make a reverse hinge. To do this, make a ½″-deep seam on the right front edge of the center panel and the left front edge of the third panel, adding to the measurements while cutting out the panels. Center hinge and stitch these seams *before* covering panels as directed above. To make sure the seams line up on the panel's edge, staple the hinge and seam allowances to the frame, keeping fabric taut and the hinge even with top and botom edges (G).

SEAMS

A nearly invisible line is formed on the right side of the fabric when two layers of fabric are stitched together and then pressed open or to one side. The seams most likely used for decorating projects are:

SECONDARY COLORS

Equal parts of two *primary colors* are mixed to make a third color. The three secondary colors are green, orange, and purple, made by mixing yellow and blue, red and yellow, and red and blue respectively.

SELF-PLEATED HEADINGS

See *Draperies,* procedure #4.

SELVAGES

These edges at each side of woven fabric are finished to prevent raveling. Usually the selvages have a different texture and sometimes a different color than the body of the fabric. Selvages have a tendency to curl and not lie flat when the seam is pressed open as it may be more taut than the body. Be sure to trim away the selvages or clip them at even intervals so they won't cause the fabric to pull at the seam or when folded into a hem.

SEW

A term used throughout this book to denote a hand-sewn operation.

SHADE

Take any of the twelve *primary, secondary,* or *tertiary* colors and add black to make a shade of that color. The more black added the darker the shade will be.

SHADES

See *Austrian Shades, Roller Shades,* or *Roman Shades,* which includes construction procedures for a Flat Roman Shade Lined #5 or Unlined #6, Reverse Tuck #7, Hobbled #8, Tuck with Eyelets #9, Balloon #10, and Cloud #11.

SHEER CURTAINS AND DRAPERIES

To make curtains and draperies from sheer fabrics, see *Curtains* or *Draperies,* procedures #1 and #3.

SHEETS

These wide seamless beauties can be a decorator's best friend. You can make a quick stationary curtain or drapery by threading a rod through the wide decorative hem after carefully removing a few stitches at the ends, if necessary. Use a pair of matching sheets the same way and tie them back with ribbon.

Make a *duvet* out of sheets to protect a down comforter, or use sheets for a comforter. To make a shower curtain, see *Bathrooms,* procedure #2. Make any of the many *curtain, drapery,* and *Roman shade* styles you will find throughout this book. Transform couches and chairs with tied-on *slipcovers,* and then add a floor-length *tablecloth* for a seasonal change.

These are just a few suggestions for using sheets. Be aware that it is almost impossible to match *pattern repeats* on sheets, so they are not recommended when this step is necessary. As you progress in your decorating skills, however, I'm sure you will find other ways to use sheets.

SHIRRING

A design feature in which two or more rows of gathering threads are used below a seam to control the fullness. See *Draperies,* procedure #10 for shirred Stationary Draperies, *Roman Shades* for the Cloud Shade, procedure #11 for a shirred top, and *Walls,* procedure #5 for an easy way to use fabric, shirred on a wall with rods.

SHOWER CURTAIN

See *Bathrooms,* procedure #2.

SHRINKAGE

The term shrinkage is used in two ways when working with decorator fabrics:

1. SHRINKAGE WHEN WASHED. For many decorator fabrics, the amount a length of fabric will shrink when washed and dried is undeterminable, so this method is not recommended for them. If you plan to make an item you want to wash, see *Shrinking Fabric* below.

2. SHRINKAGE DURING STITCHING. Shrinkage refers to the amount fabric may be reduced by *quilting,* when several layers of fabric and *batting* are stitched together; when extra full *curtains, shirred walls,* or *ruffles* need more length because the gathers make the fabric puff out; when making multiple folds such as for *bias binding,* or when rings or tape are sewn to *Roman shades.*

SHRINKING FABRIC

If you are planning to wash your bedspread, curtain, draperies, or slipcover after it is made, you need to shrink the fabric beforehand. To shrink washables, lay fabric in a large vessel of water (I use the bathtub) until thoroughly wet. Squeeze out water, do not wring, and hang over a towel bar until the fabric stops dripping. Dry fabric in dryer at proper setting, removing as soon as the fabric is dry to prevent excessive wrinkles. Or dry on a line in a wind-free area, without pins and with selvages even. Press fabric before cutting or sewing.

SHUTTERS

A form of window treatment used for privacy. Shutters are available with dowels to hold casement curtains, see *Curtains,* procedure #3.

SINK SKIRT

Sink skirts are used to gain more storage or to hide unsightly pipes. See *Bathrooms,* procedure #2.

SLACK

A term used when fabric lengths or *bias* strips hang loose or limp instead of lying smooth and flat. To remove slack before stitching, carefully stretch the fabric while pressing it lightly with a steam iron. Some fabrics may shrink or retract slightly by simply pressing them with a steam iron.

SLIP-BASTING

See *Basting,* procedure #4.

SLIPCOVERS

Traditionally, slipcovers are quite structured and therefore may be complicated. Along with a more casual lifestyle, there has evolved a simple method to make removable furniture covers. These easy slipcovers allow you to warm up furniture in cold weather, cool wooly-feeling fabrics in warm weather, change your color scheme, and hide faded or damaged fabric.

Soft or crisp fabrics may be used. Corduroy, denim, decorator fabrics, or other durable fabric will work. Be sure that the fabric is prepared in such a way that dark coverings will not show through your draped slipcover when installed.

When Measuring for a Draped Slipcover, decide whether you want the cushion and cover combined or whether you want separate cushion covers.

Slipcover and cushion combination To determine how wide the drape must be; measure from floor on one side, up to the top of the arm, across arm, down to cushion, across cushion(s), up the arm, across arm and down to the floor on the opposite side (A). Measure the depth starting at the center of the back at the floor. Measure up the back and down over the front to the cushion, across the cushion, and then down the front to the floor (B).

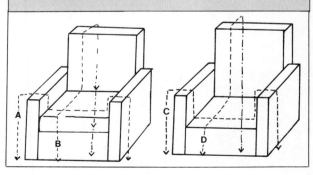

Separate slipcover and separate cushion(s): Remove cushion(s) from furniture. Disregarding reference to cushions, measure width as in step A above, measuring across the cushion deck (C). Measure depth as in step B above, measuring across cushion deck (D).

To Calculate Yardage for Draped Slipcover, add 30" to measurement A or C and 18" to measurement B or D. You will need a rectangle of fabric using these measurements. When planning the piecing, consider where the seams will fall. For most fabrics and one-way designs, use two side seams with a full fabric width at the center (see *Pattern Repeats*). Some fabrics may be used with the selvages running crosswise; piece fabric so the seam will fall across the top of the back or into the tuck at the back of the cushion.

To cover separate cushions, you will need additional fabric. See *Knife-edge Pillows,* procedure #5 for no-sew pillow and cushion covers.

To Make Slipcover, cut and stitch seams to make the fabric rectangle, rounding corners

for the gathered style. Make a 1" hem all around, using a 1½" hem allowance.

To Drape Slipcover, center fabric over furniture, with it touching the floor on each side and in front and back. Make a tuck about 6" deep between the cushion and chair, tucking fabric into the arm creases near the backrest.

For a gathered look, smooth and tuck fabric until it is draped nicely on all four sides. At the back, form excess fabric into soft folds near the top and secure invisibly with safety pins. Tie a cord around the cover just below the cushion to hold in place and distribute the fullness evenly along the cord (see the slipcover in photograph with the two-tiered café curtains).

For a more fitted look, at the arms, fold the excess fabric around to the sides and make a horizontal fold near the top of the arm. Pin layers underneath so the safety pin won't show. At the back, pull excess fabric into folds near the top and pin in place underneath. Add a tie to hold cover in place as shown in the accompaning photograph.

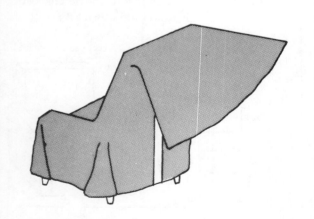

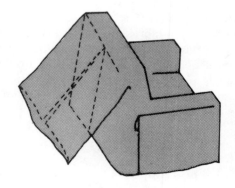

SLIP-STITCH

This durable hand-sewn stitch is used to pull two opening edges together over a flat surface; to secure two opening edges to form an edge; to sew a folded opening edge to trim on a pillow or cushion; or to attach *appliqué* or *trims*.

To start, thread needle; knot one end and bring needle up through fold on one layer. To make slip-stitches, slip needle through fold; swing needle to pick up a fiber of the thread on the opposite side (or fold). Pull up thread and repeat this step, making slip-stitches ¼" apart.

To join two flat folded edges together, turn both opening edges along the seam line; pin. Now align the two folds and slip-stitch together (A).

To form an edge on a cushion or pillow opening, turn in both edges along the seam line; pin. Next pin the two folded edges together and slip-stitch (B).

When slip-stitching an opening shut with trim, be sure to machine-stitch the trim in place along the seam line so it will be securely fastened. Turn the trim edge in along the stitching and the other edge in along the seam line. Pin folded edge in place along the stitching on the trim; slip-stitch (C).

To attach appliqué or trims, secure thread and slip needle up through the foundation. Pick up a fiber of the trim and reinsert needle. Repeat this step, making stitches in foundation about ¼" apart. Curved edges may need the stitches only ⅛" apart (D).

SNAP TAPE

The convenience of the thin twill tape with the snaps already attached makes this a quick and easy way to close an opening. Snap tape is less bulky than the nylon tape fastener with the hook and pile strips that interlock.

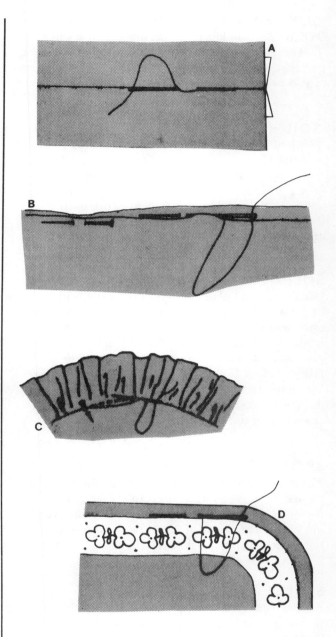

SOFT FABRIC

When selecting fabric for decorating, you will need to know how it will drape. Soft fabric will hang straight down in small soft folds when gathered on a rod or in a seam.

SOIL-RELEASE FABRICS

Most of the decorator fabrics have been treated with a finish that will protect the surface from soil. For chair arms and cushions that are used heavily, it is a good idea to spray their surfaces with a light mist of a fabric protector such as Scotchguard after the surface has been vacuumed and/or sponged off and allowed to dry thoroughly.

SOLID-COLOR FABRICS

Usually called "plain-dye fabrics" in the trade, solid-color fabrics are the foundation of decorating. On some fabrics it is difficult to tell the right side from the wrong side after the selvages have been cut away. Be sure to mark the wrong side of the fabric with a large "X" made with *tailor's chalk*. When using a solid color that reflects light in one direction, see *Nap*. *Do not* tear the fabric along the crosswise grain, see *Straightening Fabric Ends*.

SPRING TENSION RODS

These rods are secured to the window indentation by pressure. A spring is used to create tension on the ends so the rod will stay in place. Lightweight *Austrian shades, curtains,* and *Roman shades* can be hung with spring tension rods.

STABLE

A term used to denote a fabric that is firmly woven or knitted and that will not stretch in either the lengthwise or crosswise direction.

STATIONARY DRAPERIES

Any type of draperies or curtains made from *opaque* fabrics in medium- or heavy-weights and that are permanently hung. See *Draperies,* procedures #7 through #10 for lined-to-edge, tab hangers, and shirred headings. See *Tieback Curtains and Draperies* for other suggestions for making stationary draperies.

STAY-STITCHING

A term used for a row of machine-stitches made in the seam allowance alongside the seam line of inward corners and curves. This same technique is also called *reinforcement stitches.*

STIFFENING

There are several ways that stiffening is used in decorating. *Drapery* headings are stiffened with a 4"-wide, heavy stiffening made specifically for this purpose. To make scalloped tops for *café curtains* or *stationary draperies,* you may want to use an iron-on interfacing.

STITCH

A directive term used throughout this book for procedures where items are to be joined by the stitches of a sewing machine.

STRAIGHT-GRAIN STRIPS

In most cases, straight-grain strips work just as well for *cording* as the traditional *bias* strips. Use leftover fabric or purchase at least ¼ yard extra fabric.

On the wrong side of fabric, make a straight line and mark strips the necessary width. Cut along markings (A). Ends must be cut at a 45-degree angle to eliminate bulk at seam. Fold one strip diagonally with the corner up and the other with the corner down. Cut along the folds (B). Stitch ends together the same as for *Bias* strips, procedure #1, steps B and C.

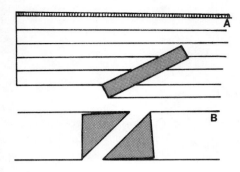

STRAIGHTENING FABRIC ENDS

To straighten the ends of *solid-color fabric,* use a T- or L-square and one yardstick or two yardsticks taped together. Align the T- or L-square with one selvage. Draw a line with *tailor's chalk* from selvage to selvage. Measure the length needed along both selvages. Draw line across fabric in the same manner. *Do not* pull a thread or tear the fabric across the crosswise grain. Modern fabrics are finished in such a way that they must be used "as is."

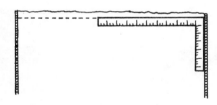

To straighten ends with a design that repeats, see *Pattern Repeats,* procedure #3.

STRIPES

Fabric with beautiful bands of color running vertically or horizontally is a decorator favorite. Stripes should be matched like any other *pattern repeats.*

STUDIO COUCH COVERS

See *Couch Covers.*

SUNBURST PILLOW COVER

See *Knife-edge Pillows,* procedure #6.

SWAGS

A garland of fabric draped across the top of a window and held in place with decorative rods, posts, or rings is called a swag. Create a soft, draping original with a scalloped center and *jabots* cascading down each side. Position hangers and measure span between and down each side of the window to the spot where the swag tips should end, adding about 12″ extra for a graceful scallop. Use soft, lightweight fabric.

Narrow hem all edges of the swag or line it by stitching two layers, the same size, together; leave an opening on one long edge to turn right side out. Stitch opening shut. Some fabrics that reflect light may need to be cut in three sections so that the *nap* will be the same on both *jabots* that hang at the sides.

When hanging swags, fold in 6″ at each hanger at the top edge to make the space taut between the hangers. This will give you more fabric on the opposite edge to shape the scallop. You may need to use strategically placed pins to hold the fabric in place and help the fabric hold its shape when the windows are opened.

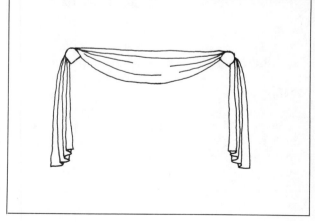

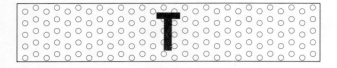

TAB

A strip of fabric, ribbon, or trim used to secure a *chair cushion;* hang café curtains, or *stationary drap-* eries on a rod. See *Curtains,* procedure #2, and *Draperies,* procedures #7 and #9, for suggestions.

TABLECLOTHS

Select permanent press fabric for tablecloths that will be used for dining and that will be washed frequently. Floor-length tablecloths can take on many looks. Make a smooth top with a gathered or pleated *drop,* use an outstanding fabric, or decorate the edges (see *Corded String Hem, Cording, Hems, Ruffles,* and *Trims*). Sheets and felt have become favorites as they seldom require piecing.

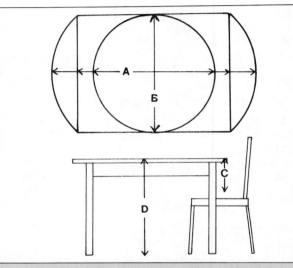

How to Measure a Table for Fabric. In order to purchase the necessary yardage for any table covering, the following measurements are needed:

Measure the length of the table at the longest point (A). Measure the width at the widest point (B). Measure to within 6″ of the chair seat for the standard drop (C). Measure from the top of the table edge to the floor for a floor-length drop (D).

To help determine yardage, add twice the drop measurement and twice the hem allowance to the actual length and width measurements. The total length and width will indicate how long the cut length will be and how many fabric widths you will need. At the store, carefully measure the length of any *pattern repeat.* Divide its measurement into the cut length requirement and purchase fabric accordingly.

When two widths are needed, cut fabric in half so each length has the same number of pattern repeats. Split one length and stitch these two sections to the wider one as shown in *Pattern Repeats,* procedure #4.

Shape Tablecloth Before Hemming: Regardless of style, the corners should be shaped before the hem is made. After the fabric has been seamed, fold fabric lengthwise, right sides together; smooth fabric to fold, keeping cut edges even. Pin cut edges together. Now fold fabric crosswise, matching folds and cut edges. Keep fabric smooth and pin cut edges, removing previous pins as you work.

For a round tablecloth, use folded corner as a pivot point. Using a yardstick, mark with a soft lead pencil one-fourth the total measurement needed. Move yardstick 1″ at a time, forming a quarter circle opposite the raw edges. Cut in a smooth circle (A).

For a square or rectangular tablecloth, measure in from the cut edges on both sides of the corner equally, the measurement of the drop plus hem allowance. Make a dot where the lines intersect. Using dot for the pivot point and the straight line measurement from the cut edge to the dot,

mark off a rounded corner. Cut off the rounded corner in a smooth line along the markings (B).

For an oval tablecloth, center fabric over table top with the wrong side uppermost, having all edges even. Weight fabric securely. With the side of a soft lead pencil or tailor's chalk, draw the shape onto the fabric along one-fourth of the edge. Fold fabric as instructed above. Using a yardstick, mark cutting line for drop. Make marks about 1″ apart. Cut along the markings in a smooth line (C).

For all shapes, finish hem edge as planned.

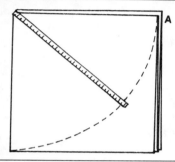
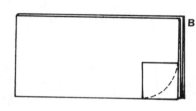
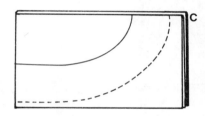

TACK

A directive term used throughout this book for a method where something is hand-sewn to another layer with several stitches.

TAILOR'S CHALK

A marking product made specifically to be used on fabric. It comes in several colors and can usually be purchased at a notions counter.

TAPE FASTENERS

There are several types of fasteners that are made with two corresponding strips and sold by the yard. See *Nylon Tape Fastener* and *Snap Tape.*

TERTIARY COLORS

Six more basic colors are made when equal parts of the *Primary* and *Secondary Colors* are mixed. Blue and green make blue-green; yellow and green make yellow-green; yellow and orange make yellow-orange; red and orange make red-orange; red and purple make violet-red; and blue and purple make blue-violet.

THROWS

A term used for decorator coverings that are created from one flat piece of fabric that has been seamed to size. This covering is thrown on the furniture and then draped or shaped to fit its contours. See *Bedspreads,* procedures #14, #15, and #16, and *Slipcovers.*

TIEBACK CURTAINS AND DRAPERIES

Expand the techniques used for *curtains*, *draperies*, *swags*, and *valances* to include tiebacks. The Priscilla curtain style, at one time seen only in sheers, is now being shown in decorator fabrics with matching and/or contrasting *cording* and *ruffles*.

Straight styles become tiebacks when they are pulled away from the center of the window in graceful folds with fabric, ribbon, or rope. These same center and side edges can be decorated with purchased *trim* (A) or you can make self- or contrasting *ruffles*. For trims that extend beyond the edges, it may be necessary to make adjustments in the length requirement (B). Be sure to add ruffle requirements to the curtain or drapery yardage.

Style variations: Tiebacks may be used with many other window treatments such as *cornices*, *lambrequins*, *swags*, and *valances*. Opening edges may meet at the center or they may be separated at the center. Separated panels may be hung on decorative rods or self-covered rods, or they can be topped with any of the treatments mentioned above.

Tiebacks may be made from trims, braids, or matching or contrasting fabric with ruffles or cording—anything that will look attractive—even colorful shoestrings for a child's room.

Tieback placement is important. Decorators fasten tiebacks one-third the curtain length from the rod or two-thirds from the floor, never in the center of the window. Make tiebacks as long or as wide as you like. Some workrooms use 4"-wide stiffening to interface the tiebacks.

To Make Tiebacks, cut two strips of fabric the length and width desired for each tieback, adding 1"–1¼" to each measurement for two ½"–⅝" seam allowances. Place two fabric strips, right sides together, then lay interfacing on top. Pin all three layers together. Stitch long edges and one end in a ½"–⅝" seam (A). Trim seam in layers and corners to eliminate bulk (B).

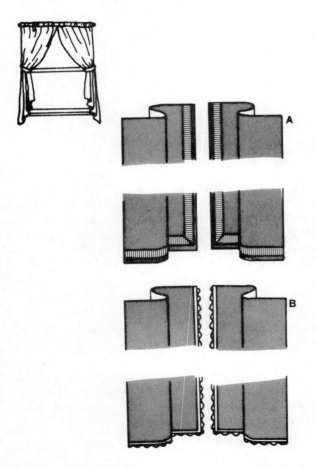

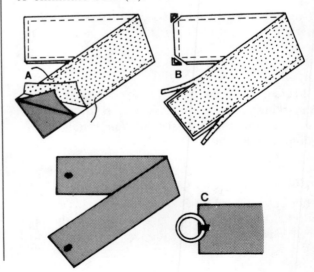

Turn right side out; press. After curtains or draperies are hung, wrap tiebacks around each panel and hold in place with a pin. Reposition or shorten tieback until the desired look is achieved. Mark position for cup hook. Tuck in raw ends and stitch folded edges together. Make buttonholes at each end or sew on rings. Anchor hook and secure tieback (C).

TINT
Add white to any of the twelve *primary, secondary,* or *tertiary colors* to make a tint of that color. The more white added, the lighter the tint will be.

TOGGLE BOLT
A screw and bolt gadget used to secure curtain and drapery fixtures to a hollow wall. See *Anchor.*

TOP-STITCH
A term used to indicate a row of machine stitches that decorate a finished edge. One or more rows may be used. Usually top-stitching is done along a finished edge, but it is sometimes used to hold a hem in place.

TRAVERSE RODS
See *Curtain and/or Drapery Rods.*

TRIM
There are two meanings to the word "trim" in decorating.

1. TRIM AS A DIRECTIVE TERM:
Indicates that some of the seam allowances and interfacing should be trimmed away to reduce bulk when the fabric is turned right side out along the seam. Trim any interfacing close to the stitching—the first fabric layer to about $\frac{1}{3}$ and make the next layer a little wider (A). Trim away corners and

points as shown (B). *Clip* inward corners and curves. (See *Clip.*) *Notch* out excess fabric along an outward curve. (See *Notch.*)

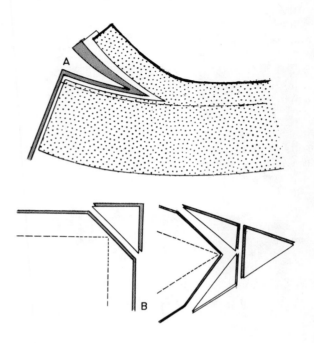

2. TRIM(S) INDICATING A DECORATION:
Trims may be used for a custom decorator touch applied to an edge as a hem finish; used to embellish the surface above the hem or finished edge; or stitched in a seam. See *Trims* below.

TRIMS
There are three types of purchased trim to use on your decorating projects: Band trims that form a colorful ribbonlike strip as a hem finish or as a decoration on the surface above the finished edge; banded trims that have a decorative free edge that extends beyond the finished edge; and decorative trims that are inserted in a seam. Also see *Bias Binding, Fold-over Braid, Cording,* and *Ruffles.*

1. BAND TRIM.
Use as a hem finish or apply to a surface for a decorator touch.

For a hem finish, turn up the raw edge ½″; press. Lap trim over raw edge with lower edge even with pressed edge. Stitch both edges in place over raw edge. *Miter* corners as directed below when applying to a surface (A). For a rounded edge, *ease* to fit (B).

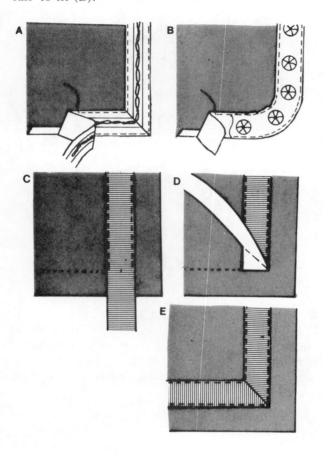

Applied to a surface: To establish the position of the trim, draw a chalk line the desired distance from the finished edge. Using the line as a guide, stitch trim to surface along both edges. To miter, end stitching at corner (C). Fold trim back at bottom edge; crease. Then fold to make a right angle; crease. Lift up trim; stitch along diagonal crease (D). Reposition trim and stitch both edges in place, covering raw edge (E). Also see *Ruffles,* procedure #3, to use a band of trim to apply a ruffle.

2. TRIM WITH AN EXTENDED FREE EDGE.

For a hem finish, apply to the edge as in step A or stitch to a surface as in step B, procedure #1 above. Miter corners (A) or ease trim around a curve (B). Insert in a seam as in procedure #3 below.

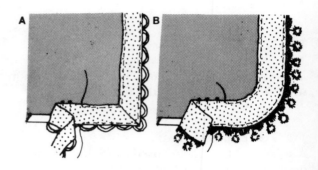

3. TRIM IN A SEAM:

To test if the trim will lie flat and smooth along the seamed edge, lay the unfinished edge along the corner, curve, or point; allow ample length so the outer decorative edge will lie flat. To apply trim to one layer, place the straight edge ⅛″ over the ½″–⅝″ seam line on the right side of the fabric. Baste trim in place, keeping decorative edge free.

For straight edges with corners or points, ease trim at corners by forming tiny pleats (A), or form a miter and stitch it to eliminate bulk. Zigzag raw edges to prevent fraying after trimming the seam to ¼″ (B).

For curved edges, ease in excess trim as you stitch by pushing tiny folds against the machine needle with a pin (C).

After trim is basted to one layer, lay trimmed layer over remaining layer, right sides together and raw edges even. Stitch the seam alongside the inner edge of the basting, leaving an opening for turning if necessary.

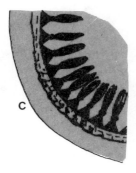

4. JOINING ENDS. Each type of trim should be joined attractively when used on a continuous edge or surface.

For band trims, turn in the upper end ½" and lap ¾" over the raw end, connecting each row of stitching as you secure the lap (A).

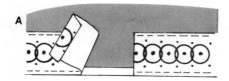

For fringe, butt ends together, making sure each end has a finished loop (B).

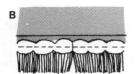

For trim stitched in a seam, turn back the first end when starting ½"; extend the remaining end ¾" as you complete the basting (C).

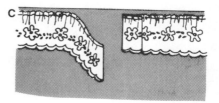

TUCKS

Small folds stitched in place may be used instead of gathers for fullness. Narrow tucks can be used to form a decorative band. Tucks may be stitched on the right side or the wrong side of the fabric. In each case, extra fabric is needed.

For a short tuck that adds fullness, stitch from outer edge to depth desired, *back-stitching* at each end of the stitching (A).

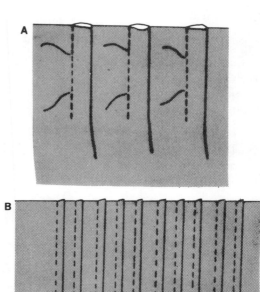

For a decorative tucked band, stitch depth of tucks as planned, then apply to a surface or hem edge (B).

TUCKS WITH EYELETS SHADE
See *Roman Shades,* procedure #9.

it is taught. There is, however, one type of upholstery that even a non-sewer can do—reupholstering flat chair seats. See *Chair Cushions,* procedure #3 for reupholstering chair seat.

UNDERLINING
Sometimes called backing, underlining can be used under lace or open-weave fabric to add color. Simply use two layers the same size, placing the wrong side of the face fabric over the right side of the underlining. *Machine-baste* the two layers together along the raw edges and handle as one layer throughout construction.

UNLINED DRAPERIES
See *Draperies,* procedure #4 for Quick Unlined Draw Draperies, #3 for Classic Unlined Draperies, and #9 for Tab Hanger Stationary Draperies.

UNLINED SHADES
See *Austrian Shades* and *Roman Shades,* procedure #6 for a Flat Unlined Shade and #11 for Cloud Shade.

UPHOLSTERED WALLS
See *Walls,* procedure #5.

UPHOLSTERY
Upholstering is best left to the experts, unless you have the time to attend a good trade school where

VALANCE
These short ornamental strips of drapery, which can help to conserve energy, may be plain, fancy, smooth, gathered, or pleated. Valances may be hung on a rod with a casing or pin hooks or stapled to a board. Make valances as narrow as 6″ or as deep as one-fifth the measurement from floor to ceiling. Line it to the edge, make a narrow or 1″ hem, and use straight or shaped edges—there are no hard-and-fast rules on how a valance must be constructed. Use any kind of heading shown throughout this book for *Curtains and Draperies*

Make a Valance Board, the same as the board used to mount a *Roman Shade,* procedure #4. Glue or staple the valance to the board. Use 2-cord or 4-cord shirr-tape for gathered styles or stitch gathers to twill tape before glueing.

Smooth valances need 2″–4″ for *shrinkage* and/or *ease* so the ends will touch the wall on each side of the return and not look skimpy. Use a casing with or without a heading to hang it on a rod or staple it to a board, distributing excess fabric evenly.

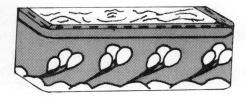

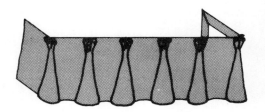

Gathered valance: Use one (A) or two rods (B) for a gathered version.

Or gather the valance and glue or staple it to a valance board. To match the fullness to the fabric weight, see *Gathers*.

Shaped valance: Make this smooth, gathered, or draped, allowing 2″–4″ for *shrinkage* and/or *ease* for the smooth style. Shaped valances are often used with café, casement, and sash curtains or draperies and may have an attached or separate *jabot*.

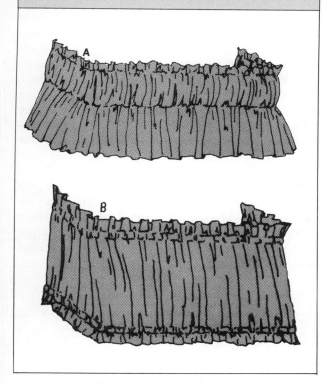

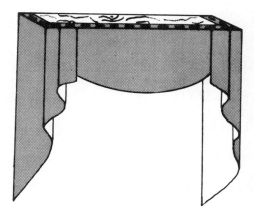

VALUE

The *shade* or *tint* is a darker or lighter value of the twelve *primary, secondary,* and *tertiary colors.*

VENT

An opening that is split or has lapped edges, allowing the item to slip on or off easily without strain.

Pleated valance: Use any style of pleat or pleater tape to make this valance. Hang on a rod with pin hooks, or fasten to the edge of a valance board.

WALL HANGINGS

A quick-and-easy way to cover a plain wall attractively is with a wall hanging. Use a fabric panel specifically designed for this use, a *pattern repeat* of a decorator fabric, a scarf, sheet, rug, or quilt. A wall hanging is an excellent way to create a focal point or camouflage a structural flaw.

Hang with two brass or wooden poles with finials, using a *casing* or *tabs* to hold the poles to stabilize the top and bottom. Frame with an artist's stretcher frame or make your own frame as directed in *Screens.*

WALLS

There are two comparatively easy ways to cover walls with fabric. Upholstered walls have fabric stapled over batting; shirred walls are made like casement curtains. Both methods will cover cracked or damaged walls and go over wallpaper, wood paneling, brick, cinder blocks, or rough-textured walls. Cover one wall for a focal point, or do all four. Upholstered walls will add some insulation and cut down on the noise because of the batting. Shirred walls will also absorb some noise. Fabric on bathroom walls may mildew in some homes without proper ventilation.

Start small with one wall or behind your bed as an accent and then work up to a whole room. Don't start with a "powder room" just because it is small. Powder rooms have too many corners and pipes and cabinets to work around.

1. ROOM STRUCTURE AND FABRIC SELECTION. Wall construction and fabrics should be considered regardless of the size of your project.

Find out if walls will receive staples or hold rods easily. Make a test with a staple gun as some dry and cinder-block walls have metal meshing in corners that cannot be stapled. You may want to pound a nail to test for screw placement. For most walls, you won't have a problem. To upholster walls that cannot be stapled, you will need furring strips (see procedure #4 below). Usually you can place rod fixtures on a stud. To anchor screws in a masonry wall, you will need a special drill bit to drill a hole to anchor screws. Think about the fabric you plan to use. Solid-color fabrics will not have the impact of prints, large or small, unless they have surface interest such as moiré, taffeta, and velvet. Any kind of medium-weight decorator fabric—florals, scenes, or random geometrics—work well. Avoid designs that have vertical and horizontal impact that may accent uneven ceilings or corners. Prints in an all-over design and predominant pattern repeats work best. Vertical stripes are eye-catching in wall upholstery if they are straight and taut. Large-scale prints should be centered between windows or doors on a major wall that will be a part of the focal point. Measurements for special placement may change yardage requirements. When in doubt about your choice, ask the store if you can take the fabric out on approval, so you can see it in your room.

For upholstered walls, a whole pattern repeat should start at the ceiling as this is the most visible area, allowing a ½″ turnunder above the predominant motif. For shirred walls, gather a length of fabric in your hand to see how it will look shirred. See *Pattern Repeats.*

2. MEASURING AND YARDAGE WORK SHEET: To calculate fabric and batting yardage, measure width of each wall from corner to corner (A), (B), (C), and (D) in inches, disregarding any window or doors. Measure height from ceiling to wallboard (E).

Width of each wall,   A _____

   corner to corner   +B _____

                                                            +C _____

                                                            +D _____

   Equals room perimeter   = _____

Determine the number of fabric widths needed:

For upholstered walls procedure #3, divide perimeter by fabric width: 36",
  44", 48", 54", 60"   ÷ _____

Equals number of fabric widths   = _____

For shirred walls procedure #5, multiply perimeter for double fullness   × ____2____

Equals adjusted perimeter   = _____

Divide by fabric width: 36", 44", 48", 54", 60"   ÷ _____

Equals number of fabric widths   = _____

Determine the cut length, for each fabric width required:

For upholstered walls, measurement E   _____

Add 3½ " allowance   + _____

Equals cut length   = _____

For shirred walls, measurement E

Add amount needed for two casings and shrinkage   + _____

Equals cut length   = _____

   For fabric with pattern repeat:

   Divide cut length by *pattern repeat* length   ÷ _____

   Equals number of repeats per length. If fraction remains round up to next full
    number   = _____

   Multiply by length of repeat   × _____

   Equals adjusted cut length   = _____

For both styles, multiply the cut length   _____

Times number of fabric widths   × _____

Equals yardage in inches   = _____

Divided by 36   ÷ ___36___

Equals total yardage required   = _____

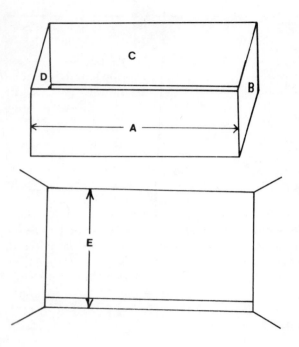

3. UPHOLSTERED WALLS. These elegant fabric-covered walls got their name because some of the techniques were adapted from upholstering. The fabric is sewn in one continuous piece and stretched over batting stapled to the wall for padding. The fabric is attached to the walls with staples along the ceiling, baseboard, around windows and doors, and at inward corners. The rest of the fabric is smooth and taut without a wrinkle. Staples are hidden with a decorative trim—the professional choice is self- or contrasting fabric covered double welting, see *Welting,* procedure #2.

Use bonded polyester fiberfill *batting,* ⅝"–1" thick, available by the yard. Cotton batting does not hold up and gets lumpy. Thinner batting will not give an elegant padded look.

Assemble Materials and Equipment Needed: Before you purchase anything for upholstered walls, carefully review procedures #1 and #2.

Materials: Fabric and batting yardage, including additional yardage for double welting if you do not have a lot of leftover fabric from windows and doors. Two strands of cord the length of the baseboard and ceiling perimeter, the length of each window and door opening perimeter, measurement of counter top and sides, and all inward corners of all the walls and soffits. (The average room needs approximately 30 yards of double welting, requiring 60 yards of cord.) Matching thread.

Equipment: Plumbline or substitute and chalk. Pushpins. Staple gun and staples. Glue gun and glue sticks, or quick-drying white fabric glue. Sewing machine. Scissors. Single-edge razor blades or mat knife. Thin, flat-head screwdriver. Stepladder or stool that will enable you to reach the ceiling.

Before You Start: Remove all objects from the walls —nails, screws, light switch, and outlet plates. Brackets used to hold heavy mirrors, lamps, and towel bars or other bathroom fixtures should be left in place. It is impossible to drill or screw through batting and fabric as they will twist the fabric and batting and distort or tear the fabric. Use molly bolts with points to hang anything on fabric, carefully making a small slit and pushing the batting away from the area.

Start with Batting: Start at one inward corner. Staple every 10"–12" along ceiling through all thicknesses about ½"–¾" below the cut edge and along the baseboard the same way. Using scissors, cut away batting. Staple the next strip in place at the ceiling and baseboard, butting the side edges snugly together. Where the two strips are butted, separate the top half of the batting on each strip and staple the inner halves together and to the wall. Coax batting over staples, making it look continuous.

For inward corners, staple on each wall that forms the corner.

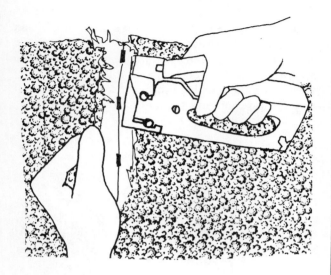

For outward corners, simply wrap batting around the corner; *do not* staple along either of its edges. Cover all the walls in this manner.

Windows, doors, and electrical outlets: Staple around window edges the same as for ceiling and baseboard, cutting away batting as you work. Do doors, electrical outlets, and retained brackets the same way. Piece batting by the butting

method, so the joinings won't show up as shadows or indentations after the fabric is attached.

For extra-high walls, you may want to bury staples at one-third and two-thirds the length by opening the batting and stapling the inner half. This will help prevent dimples from showing through where the staples were placed.

Establish Plumbline: First decide where the first panel should start. In most cases it is wise to start in an inconspicuous corner when doing a whole room, but for one wall, a fabric width should be centered on the center of the wall.

Since walls are rarely squared, you need a line to start your first panel. Use a strong string, colored chalk, a plumb bob or other heavy object, and a pushpin. Secure a length of chalked line at the ceiling with the heavy object nearly touching the floor. Holding string taut, pull it out and snap it against the batting for a true vertical line.

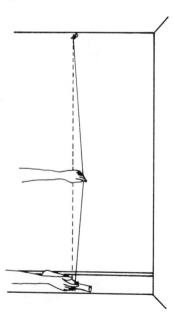

Joining Fabric Widths: Cut all fabric lengths, drawing a cutting line as explained in *Pattern Repeats,* procedures #2 and #3, making sure you allowed the extra 3″ for uneven walls or floors.

The following one-step matching and stitching process, used by professionals, eliminates pressing and slip-basting: Place the two fabric widths right sides together as you would for a regular seam. Turn back selvages on top layer until the pattern is aligned on both. Pin at several spots, close to the fold, along these edges. Check the right side to see how the pattern is matched, making any adjustments needed. Keeping fabric taut, stitch as close to fold as possible. Check pattern repeat on the right side to make sure the pattern matches before completing the whole seam.

Hang with pushpins: Starting in an inconspicuous corner or at the center of a single wall, line up first seam with plumb line. Fold down ½", wrong sides together, and hold in place along the ceiling edge with pushpins. Step back to see it the fabric is hanging straight and right side out.

Clip selvages every 2" or trim away if the printing shows through on the right side of the fabric.

Attaching Fabric to Wall: Join all fabric widths as explained above for matching pattern repeats, leaving one seam open. Press out any sharp creases; soft wrinkles can be smoothed out when the fabric is stretched over the batting. Hang fabric loosely along the perimeter of each wall with pushpins to prevent further wrinkling.

Staple ceiling and inward corners: Smooth fabric along ceiling and extend side edges 1" beyond corner. Make fabric taut, but not stretched, and staple along the ceiling of one wall. Place staples about 2" apart for most fabrics. Soft fabrics such as silk or moiré taffeta need the staples placed end to end to prevent ripples radiating between the staples.

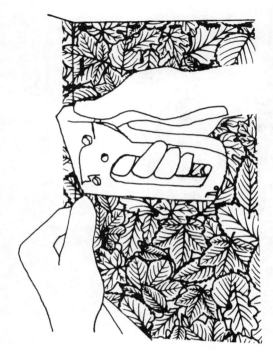

Cut Away Fabric: At doors and windows, place a pushpin at each corner or along a shaped edge, then mark the outline. Starting at the center, cut diagonally to each corner. Trim fabric to a workable 1″ length. Turn in raw edge and staple as close to opening as possible.

Work along one wall first. Starting at the center of the wall, smooth fabric over batting to the baseboard, taking out the slack. Anchor with pushpins and work out to each corner. For inward corners, staple vertically on each side of the corner near the fold formed in the corner crease. The two rows of staples should be as close as possible so they can be covered by double welting.

Staple along baseboard, ignoring any openings that have been covered. The last thing you do is to cut away any fabric over doors and windows, after the inward corners are stapled and the outward corners are smooth and flat. Fabric *must* be taut: Press your fingers against the fabric. If any indentations remain, pull out the staples carefully and stretch fabric a little tighter.

To remove excess fabric, take a blunt object such as a flat-head screwdriver and force fabric into the crack between the wall and the baseboard. Cut away fabric with a razor blade or mat knife.

For electrical outlets and switches, locate area with pushpins. Staple fabric so that the staples won't be seen when plate is installed. Turn off power and carefully cut away fabric.

Cover electrical plates with fabric that matches the fabric on the wall. Put glue on front of plate and hold in position. Center fabric, aligning pattern with wall. Wrap fabric to underside of plate and glue in place. Pierce fabric over openings and make diagonal cuts to corners. Glue these edges to underside. Take tip of scissors and pierce at screw holes, without breaking fibers if possible.

To Cover Staples, make double welting as explained for *Welting,* procedure #2, or use a selected alternate finish. To attach welting, use a glue gun or white fabric glue. Place a thin line of glue on back of welting strip for 12″–18″. Starting at the ceiling in a corner, glue a vertical strip of welting over staples. Using a thin, flat-head screwdriver, press welting down in the center between the cords and into the corner. Do all vertical rows first that extend from ceiling to floor or counter tops. This also includes any areas such as a doorway that starts and ends at the baseboard. For the white glue, you may need to hold welting in place with pushpins; the hot glue from the gun adheres almost instantly.

Apply welting to ceiling and baseboard edges in the same manner, easing welting into corners with a screwdriver. Butt ends together so the cord does not show where they meet.

4. FURRING STRIP INSTALLATION: Purchase the ¼″-thick furring strips at a lumber store. Attach strips with nails designed for your type of wall or glue them in place with paneling adhesive. Attach furring strips along the ceiling, baseboard, windows, and inward corners wherever the metal mesh corner pieces were used. Other types of walls such as masonry may need a furring under each width of batting where the side edges are butted together.

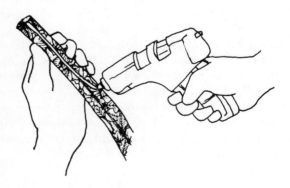

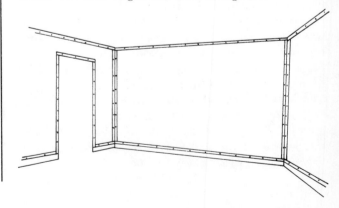

5. SHIRRED WALLS: For a soft decorator touch, use yards of fabric gathered between two curtain rods for a dramatic way to cover up cracked, patched, or peeling walls. Cover a wall or two with an eye-catching fabric or use a light-colored fabric in a dark room. Light- to medium-weight soft fabrics work best.

Shirred walls are made exactly like casement curtains, procedure #3 in *Curtains*. Use sash rods or café curtain rods that have brackets that will hold the fabric close to the wall, or farther out from the wall to hide pipes, trims, etc. Place rods 1½" from floor and ceiling (A).

Make a *casing* with a 1½" heading and a casing wide enough to accommodate the rod with a ½" turnunder to finish the casing. To measurement E in procedure #2, *Measuring and Yardage Work Sheet* at the beginning of this section on walls, add 1" for shrinkage to allow for fabric take-up when it is shirred on the rods, two 1½" headings for the top and bottom, and twice the amount needed for casing and a ½" turnunder. Example: Add 8" (3" for the backside of two 1½" headings, 3" for two 1½" casings, 1" for two ½" turnunders, 1" for shrinkage).

Cut Panels: Cut each fabric length as required. It is not necessary to stitch all fabric widths together, simply turn in the fabric along the line where the pattern repeats would match, including the selvage; press. These edges will not show when the fabric is shirred on the rod.

Make Casings: Turn in both ends where the fold of the heading should be; press. Make casing with a heading, stitching 1½" from fold. Turn under raw edge of casing ½"; stitch in place (B).

Insert rod through top casing and push tight together to form creases and shirring along rod (C). Hang rod with fabric on top rod(s). Support rods with L-screws if the fabric's weight makes rod bow. Insert rod in bottom and stretch the fabric taut. Mark position for bracket and install upside down to hold fabric taut. Secure rod(s) to brackets. Distribute shirring evenly along each rod so fabric is in smooth vertical folds. Tuck pressed edges into the folds.

To expose light switches, you may want to remove the plate and staple fabric to wall, covering plate with matching fabric the same as for upholstered walls under the section for electrical switches and outlets.

Hang pictures from wires hooked to the rod or place a nail between panels.

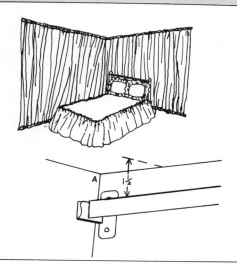

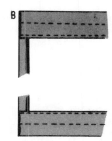

WEIGHTS

See *Draperies,* procedure #6.

WELTING

A strengthening or ornamental finish along a seam or an edge. Welting is a term sometimes used incorrectly for *cording.*

1. TO STRENGTHEN A SEAMED EDGE. Welting is formed by stitching a narrow seam, right sides together. Next, turn the fabric right side out along the stitching and press the edge flat. Now add a row of stitches from the pressed edge, through all thicknesses, encasing the raw edges.

This finish is ornamental, too. See *Garment Bags* and *Knife-edge Pillows,* procedure #3, for projects with welting formed by stitching.

2. DOUBLE WELTING: This decorative ornamental trim is used by upholsterers and is most effective on *Walls,* procedure #3, for upholstered walls.

Cut 2¾" wide *bias strips* or *straight-grain strips.* It is not necessary to use true bias for double welting unless the fabric's pattern will be more effective cut on the bias.

Lay one strand of cord near the center of the strip (A). Fold fabric over cord so the edges meet (B).

Place second strand of cord next to the first strand (C). Fold both fabric layers back over the second row of cord; pin in place to get started.

To stitch, use the wide zigzag presser foot and center the two strands of cord equally with the needle piercing the center and not catching the cords in the stitching. Use a longer stitch and adjust the tension, if necessary, so the stitches lie smooth on both sides. Trim off any excess fabric that shows from the right side (D). Stitching from the back will cup the fabric around the cords on the front (E).

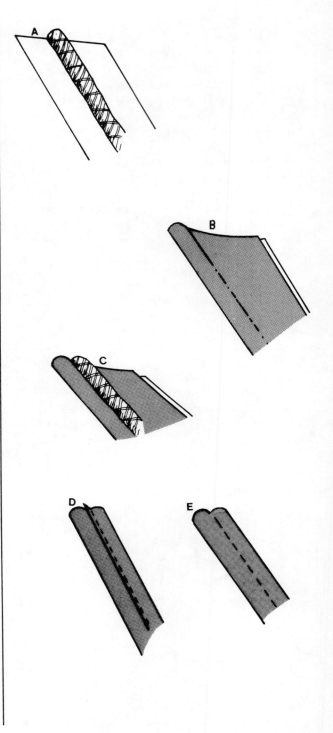

WINDOWS

For all kinds of window fashions, see *Austrian Shades; Cornices; Curtains* for Straight, Café, Casement, and Hourglass Curtains; *Draperies* for Draw and Stationary styles; *Lambrequins; Roller Shades; Roman Shades* with lined or unlined Flat, Reverse Tucks, Hobbled, Tucks with Eyelets, Balloon and Cloud styles; *Screens; Swags; Tieback Curtains and Draperies,* and *Valances.*

To measure for these various window treatments, see *Measuring Windows.*

ZIPPER CLOSURES

Throughout this book you will find projects with zipper closures. See *Bolsters,* procedures #1, #2, or #3; *Box-edge Cushions,* procedures #1 or #2; *Garment Bags; Knife-edge Pillows,* procedure #2.

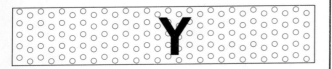

YARDAGE GUIDE

When calculating yardage for your decorating, use this simple guide to help you understand the various increments by which fabric is sold.

⅛ yard	=	4½ "
¼ yard	=	9"
⅜ yard	=	13½ "
½ yard	=	18"
⅝ yard	=	22½ "
¾ yard	=	27"
⅞ yard	=	31½ "
1 yard	=	36"